THE
FIRST FLORIDA
CAVALRY
REGIMENT
C.S.A.

THE
FIRST FLORIDA
CAVALRY
REGIMENT
C.S.A.

CHARLIE C. CARLSON

Published by
LUTHERS
New Smyrna Beach, Florida

Published by

LUTHERS PUBLISHING

1009 North Dixie Freeway

New Smyrna Beach, FL 32168-6221

PRINTED IN THE UNITED STATES OF AMERICA

LIBRARY OF CONGRESS
CATALOGING-IN-PUBLICATION DATA
Carlson, Charlie C., 1943 –
The First Florida Cavalry Regiment C.S.A. /
Charlie Carlson – 1st ed.
p.   cm.
ISBN 1-877633-43-7
Includes bibliographical references (p.   ) and index.
1. Confederate States of America. Army.
Florida Cavalry Regiment, 1st.
2. United States–History–Civil War,
1861-1865–Regimental histories.
3. Florida–History–Civil War,
1861-1865–Regimental histories.
4. Confederate States of America. Army.
Florida Cavalry Regiment. 1st Registers.
5. Soldiers–Florida Registers. I. Title.

E558.6 1st.C37 1999   99-21317
973.7' 459–dc21   CIP

CONTENTS

☆☆☆☆◨◨◨◨◨◨◨◨◨◨◨◨◨◨☆☆☆☆

dedicated to

WILLIAM CHARLES HAWKINS
PRIVATE, C.S.A.

1843-1907

William Charles Hawkins was born in Leon County, Florida, in 1843. During the third Seminole war, his parents, William Sr. and Mary Cox-Hawkins, relocated the family to Manatee County. With the outbreak of the Civil War, 19 year old William volunteered for duty with a coast guard militia patrolling Tampa Bay and Florida's Gulf Coast.

In January 1862, he saddled up his cow pony and rode off to join Company K, of the First Florida Cavalry Regiment. As a private, he served in all of the Regiment's major battles and campaigns, and was wounded during the Battle of Dallas, Georgia. He was one of only a few original volunteers still with the Regiment when it surrendered in 1865.

After the war, he settled in northwest Orange County, { the part which is now Seminole County}, and was one of the area's first cattlemen. He was an original member of Sanford's Masonic Lodge and established one of the area's first meat processing businesses. In 1875, he married Marquita Victoria Metts and together they raised nine children.

William Charles Hawkins died in 1907 and is buried next to his wife, in the old Sylvan Lake Cemetery, near Paola, west of Sanford, Florida.

☆☆☆☆◨◨◨◨◨◨◨◨◨◨◨◨☆☆☆☆

CHAPTER ONE

A CALL TO ARMS

On January 10, 1861, Florida became the third state to succeed from the Union. Florida was hardly prepared for war, its arsenal contained only enough arms to outfit a its few militia companies. While the Militia Law of 1859 had provided a sufficient strength of officers, the organized state militia was severely weak in men, training, and equipment. During the first half of 1861, as war became imminent, there was an expeditious effort, state-wide, to raise and organize volunteer companies. Governor Madison Perry, on February 4, 1861, stated to the General Assembly, that legislators *"had the duty to protect the sovereignty of the state."* The governor, although realizing that Florida could not rally a very large military force, proclaimed, *"We should proceed to organized the force which we are likely to be called upon to furnish."* On February 14th, a law was passed authorizing Florida's civil war militia. The governor, however, found himself faced with the financial problem of trying to arm and equip these new troops. There were expectations that the Confederacy would provide logistical support to Florida's troops, at least those requisitioned for regular service. But, financial and logistical troubles would remain a critical problem for the state's forces throughout the war. Counties all around the state began organizing their own volunteer companies. Men of all ages flocked to enroll in local units while community women and church groups began making uniforms, tents, and flags, to properly outfit their boys.

In April 1861, William George Mackey Davis, a wealthy forty-nine year old Tallahassee lawyer and land owner, gave 50,000 dollars to the state for raising Florida's first infantry regiment. Davis, a distant cousin of President Jefferson Davis, in June 1861, began raising his own independent company of cavalry in Tallahassee. When the state authorized tax exemptions on personal horses and equipment of *"state mounted men"* or *"members of state cavalry,"* mounted companies began springing up all over Florida. William M. Footman, in July 1861, formed a mounted company from around Leon County and proposed to offer his men to Davis' cavalry.

William G. M. Davis had received authority from the secretary of war to raise a battalion of cavalry, with the assurance that it would be mustered into Confederate service. In the meantime, Davis would establish his headquarters and camp of instruction, six miles from Tallahassee at Camp Mary Davis, so named for his wife, Mary Elizabeth Mills Davis. Officially, William G. M. Davis, at this point, held no a rank, although he was socially referred to as *"Colonel"* and often used the title when signing documents.

By July 1861, William M. Footman's small company, camped on his property at Camp Footman in Leon County, had started drilling instruction. In nearby Columbia County, Captain Arthur Roberts was pledging to raise another mounted company for Davis' battalion.

In June 1861, William G. M. Davis' small unit was called *Davis' First Florida Cavalry Company*. There have been several organizations to use the designation of First Florida Cavalry. Prior to seccession, an earlier

1.

militia unit, commanded by Colonel George T. Ward, was called the First Regiment of Florida Cavalry. Near the close of the war, in September 1864, the Union organized their own First Regiment of Florida Cavalry, USA, by offering six hundred dollar bounties to enlistees recruited mainly from *"Confederate refugees and deserters."* In addition, there was also a First East Florida Cavalry, USA, organized for federal service in Florida. Because of the similarity in names, the Confederate units are often confused with the Union organizations. Another Confederate mounted unit, unrelated to Davis' organization, although sometimes referred to as the *"First Florida Cavalry,"* was the Florida First Special Cavalry Battalion; organized in late 1864. This short lived unit was organized to guard cattle drives in Florida and also went by the names, *"Cow Cavalry or Cattle Guards,"* and *"Special Commissary Battalion."*

The lineage of the First Florida Cavalry Regiment, CSA, can be indirectly connected to an earlier militia group. A few of the first enrollees of Davis' First Florida Cavalry Company had originally belonged to Captain William T. Stockton's mounted militia, the *Gadsen Dragoons*. After first offering his dragoons for state service, Stockton decided to disband his company and seek an appointment in the Confederate army. With his superior military background, William Stockton was destined to play a prominent role in the First Cavalry Regiment. Captain Stockton, in 1834, had graduated eighth in his class at West Point, where he was retained as an artillery instructor. As a United States Army officer, he had served as both an artillery and engineer officer. Following his service in the Seminole War at Tampa Bay, he was reassigned to command the defensive works at the mouth of the Black River on Lake Ontario. In 1844, he was a captain in the Florida Cavalry until 1846, when he was elected lieutenant colonel and put in charge of the State Cavalry. He was appointed Adjutant General and Inspector General of Florida in 1849 while continuing to command his own mounted militia until succession. As a result of Governor Perry's recommendation to the secretary of war, William Stockton was appointed to the rank of captain in the Confederate army. After receiving his appointment, in May 1861, as an infantry captain, Stockton was assigned to the First Florida Cavalry. In July, he was promoted to major and detached on mustering duty. During this period he was responsible for enrolling many of Florida's first companies into their respective regiments.

In a letter from the secretary of war, dated September 6, 1861, William G. M. Davis was informed that if he raised a fully equipped and armed, mounted regiment, with a compliment of officers, then his unit would be accepted into Confederate service for 12 months. Under this authority Davis proceeded to organize eight companies from various counties of the state. He was also informed that two additional companies were being organized in Alachua and Hillsborough counties. Davis notified these companies that if they could meet sufficient company strength, that he would accept them in order to bring his battalion up to regimental size.

In October 1861, after waiting nearly a year to take office, John Milton succeeded Madison Perry as Governor of Florida. Governor-elect Milton inherited his predecessor's military financial and logistical problems. From the very beginning Milton had strongly opposed raising cavalry companies. The new governor argued with just about every politician and military leader, from Jefferson Davis down to Colonel William Davis, that cavalry would present an unnecessary burden on the state. He believed that only infantry and artillery were needed to defend the state's 1700 miles of coast. He predicted that *"every man who had a pony would want to mount him at government expense."* Milton, with good reason, believed that enlistees, who would otherwise join infantry companies, would now flock to the cavalry ranks. The idea of being a mounted warrior appealed to the ego; of course for many, riding to war had to be better than walking. The governor pointed out the excessive cost of maintaining mounted units, which required saddles, feed, farrier services, and various other logistical needs not normally associated with regular infantry units. Milton conveyed his argument in a letter to President Jeff Davis. The president concurred with the governor and responded that he was surprised that the previous secretary of war had issued authority to William Davis for raising a mounted regiment. On October 25th, the president assured Governor Milton that he would *"inquire about what has been done with a view to correct what must be a misapprehension on the part of the recruiting officer."* Obviously the president had more pressing matters since Governor Milton never received any further response concerning the issue. In the meantime, William Davis ignored the governor's arguments and went on with organizing his cavalry battalion. [Note: There were some speculations that W.G.M.Davis, being a distant relative of the president, had received "*favored attention*" from the War Department].

In October 1861, William Stockton began his duty of mustering in the companies of the First Florida Cavalry, some of which had started their recruiting efforts as early as May 1861. On October 3, 1861, Arthur Roberts' group from Columbia County became the first company mustered into the First Florida Cavalry Battalion. This unit, with 68 men, was mustered into service at Lake City and designated as Company "A." Captain Stockton then proceeded to Jacksonville where he signed into service Captain John G. Haddock's mounted volunteers, mostly from Nassau County. Haddock's 90 men became Company "B." Back in Leon County, Davis and Footman continued recruiting for their companies as Stockton headed for Sanderson to inspect the readiness of Captain John Harvey's 63 men from Baker County. Harvey's men were enrolled as Company "D" on October 16th at the courthouse in Sanderson. John Harvey, who had held several elected positions in county government, including county judge and commissioner, had served as a militia captain during the second Seminole War. In a ceremony, fitting the occasion, the local ladies of Sanderson presented the company with a homemade flag inscribed with, *"God Armeth Us."* In honor of these hometown volunteers, Mrs. F. J. Fonce addressed a large crowd gathered at the courthouse, *"Soldiers, you are brave boys, who volunteered in defense of our rights and our liberties, go forth! You have before you as your leader, a brave, experienced commander. Remember the flag."* In response, as he accepted the flag, Captain Harvey remarked, *"It shall not be forgotten; and while gazing upon it we will remember the loved ones at home, hoping for the time soon to come when we may be enabled to return home, bringing with us the flag untarnished to the tender hands who made it and tendered it to us.*" Such scenes, as the one in Sanderson, were repeated across Florida as proud volunteers were mustered into companies. In Middleburg, on October 17th, Captain John A. Summerlin's 62 Clay County volunteers, with 70 horses, officially became "C" Company.

During November 1861, Major Stockton mustered four more mounted companies into the First Florida Cavalry. On November 9, 1861, Captain William D. Clark's company from Alachua County, consisting of 62 men, was mustered in as Company "G." On November 14th, Captain Charles Cone's company from Suwannee County, with 71 men, was enrolled as Company "E." On November 16th, Captain William M. Footman's company was signed up as Company "F," which after merging with Davis' original company of Leon County enrollees, had a total strength of 36 mounted men. On November 23rd, Captain Noble Hull's 46 troops from Duval County, were mustered in as Company "H."

The First Florida Cavalry, now with eight companies, a total of about 500 enrollees, under the command of William G. M. Davis, was redesignated the *First Florida Cavalry Battalion*. On November 4th, William G. M. Davis, as battalion commander, was appointed to the rank of lieutenant-colonel in the provisional Confederate army.

Although Lt. Colonel Davis had succeeded in putting together his cavalry battalion as proposed, Governor Milton was still opposing the use of mounted troops in defending Florida. In another communiqué to Secretary of War, J. P. Benjamin, the governor complained that the First Cavalry was ill equipped and that the state could not afford to maintain them. He suggested that the Confederate government should equip the unit, or *"otherwise they should be disbanded or converted to infantry."* In a following letter, Milton argued that Lt. Colonel Davis' battalion was unfit for service and with that being the case, the government *"was under no obligation to honor the previous assurance to Davis."* The governor was referring to the special authority given to Davis by the War Department, to raise a cavalry regiment. The governor, for whatever reasons, brought up to the secretary of war, that William Davis had *"originally opposed the succession of Florida and was now commanding Florida troops."*

By December 1861, the companies of the First Florida Cavalry Battalion had assembled at Camp Mary Davis for organization and instruction. The enlistees, severely lacking in arms and essential equipment, had to drill using sticks as make-believe rifles. Most of the troops had some semblance of a uniform, thanks to a limited quartermaster issue and the sewing efforts of hometown ladies. For the most part, camp life was filled with much idle time, which for a few, caused an urge to sneak off to home. One of the most difficult aspects of soldiering for the recruits was military discipline. Most resented being *"ordered around,"* which according to one private, *"took a bit of getting use to."* Lt. Colonel Davis was strictly military and according to one newspaper article, he demanded *"strict dress and discipline,"* and would not talk directly with the enlisted ranks. Colonel Davis would communicate only through his chain-of-command and expected no less from his officers and their sergeants.

The men furnished their own horses and tack, with the understanding that the government would provide a monthly allowance for horses. The government had furnished only a few wagon mules. It is estimated that the battalion had about four baggage wagons on December 1, 1861 at Camp Mary Davis. These were likely furnished by Davis, however each company later had its own baggage wagon. At one point in 1862, the First Cavalry had at least two blacksmith wagons and one headquarters baggage wagon. Later, during the campaigns, army wagons were furnished by the higher commands under which the unit was assigned. Based on various methods of estimating, [such as the number of teamsters, requisitions for feed, fodder, tack, and etc] the First Cavalry usually had between eight and twelve wagons. Later in 1863, there is a soldier's comment about the unit having *"kept some wagons we had captured."* During the Florida operations of 1862, the Regiment relied mainly on the railroad between Tallahassee and Callahan for transportation of its baggage and supplies.

At both Camp Mary Davis and Camp Footman, recruits had sufficient tenting, or other "quarters," which provided adequate shelter. The food provisions were fair and *"quantities of beef and meal were requisitioned at the depot for the First Cavalry."* Messing equipment had been issued to the men and cooking duties were shared in assigned groups of 15 men, called "messes." Individuals were responsible for their personal eating equipment, but shared the burden, as complained one private, of *"toting the mess kettle."* The kettle served as the central cooking pot for each mess.

Those having certain required skills were often assigned to special details or additional duties. Each company had a detailed farrier, blacksmith, bugler, and teamsters for driving the wagons. There were eleven known musicians attached to the headquarters' staff. During the first year of organization, the First Cavalry had a small band. Later, in mid-1862, the Regiment's muscians were attached to brigade level bands. Each company had an assigned bugler during the first year of the war. The Regiment also used drummer boys until early 1862, the exact number is not known and apparently, most were later discharged for being underage or reassigned to brigade bands.

On December 1, 1861, Captain Nicholas S. Cobb's 35 man company from Levy County became Company "I" of the First Florida Cavalry Battalion. [Note: *Some accounts have erroneously reported this company as being from Alachua County and commanded by Captain Clark, while recording Clark's Company "G" as being from Levy County and commanded by Nicholas Cobb*].

The First Cavalry Battalion officially entered the war in December 1861, when it was assigned to the Department of Middle and Eastern Florida, under the command of Brigadier-General J. H. Trapier. In a December 1861 letter, Trapier requested instructions from the Adjutant General in Richmond concerning the status of the First Florida Cavalry. Trapier was caught up in the arguements between Florida's governor, the War Department, and Lt. Colonel Davis, about disbanding, or retaining, the unit for Confederate service. On December 24th, J. P. Benjamin, secretary of war, responded by upholding the initial commitment made to Colonel Davis about raising a cavalry regiment, and added, *"If these troops*

[Davis' cavalry] *are not needed in Florida, order the Regiment at once to Bowling Green to report to General A. S. Johnston.*" But, General Trapier needed the First Cavalry to reinforce defenses in East Florida and ordered Lt. Colonel Davis to move his battalion to Camp Trapier, near Callahan.

Governor Milton, in a December 30th letter to the secretary of war, predicted, *"...that in less than two months* {Gen. Trapier} *will be more anxious to get rid of what is known as Davis' Cavalry Regiment than he was to receive it. It will prove useless and vastly expensive."* Once again, the governor restated that Florida could not equip the Regiment and since Davis' cavalry had been sanctioned by the Confederate government, then the government should be responsible for properly outfitting the troops as cavalry, *"with carbines, sabers, and pistols."*

On January 1, 1862, Captain David Hughes' enlistees were mustered into service at Ichepuckesassa [Plant City] as Company "K." This company had enrolled 51 men from the rural cattle region around Hillsborough County. Many of these men were South Florida cowmen, skilled horsemen who were at home in the saddle. Some had previously served in a local coast guard militia patrolling the Gulf coast. According to one account, from Private William Charles Hawkins, these men did not report to the camp of instruction at Camp Davis, instead, they rode by horseback to Jacksonville and later joined the Battalion at Camp Trapier. In addition to having traveled the farthest distance, Company "K" was also the last company mustered into the First Florida Cavalry. With the enrollment of Hughes' company, the Battalion was redesignated as the First Florida Cavalry Regiment C.S.A. William G. M. Davis, now a regimental commander, was promoted to full colonel, with Lt. Colonel George Troupe Maxwell serving as his second-in-command, and Major William T. Stockton, as the primary regimental field officer.

The ten companies of the Regiment initially had an estimated combined strength of about 586 rank and file. Of the original enlistees, a significant number were soon discharged for age or physical problems, but were replaced by new enlistments and transfers from other units. The highest personnel strength reached by the Regiment was 999 during the Spring of 1862. However, during the life of the Regiment, an estimated 1100 soldiers, at one time, or another, served with the unit. Some served for only a day, while a few endured to the end of the war. Exact counts are made difficult due to transfers, discharges, detachments, attachments, consolidations, casualties, desertions, and of course, lost records.

In noting the alphabetical order of the companies, one quickly finds that "Company J" is missing from the Regiment. Although there was an old soldier superstition which claimed that "J" was an unlucky letter, the actual absence of a "J" company had more to do with preventing confusion in military administration. Since "J" and "I" were easily confused in early handwriting styles, the American armies traditionally did not use "J" as a company designation.

The enlistees, motivated by the spirit of glory and willingness to defend their home state, had, for the most part, marched off to war in their well worn civilian clothes complimented with homemade parts of uniforms, but few were fortunate enough to have a complete government issued uniform.

One private, who was later issued a regular uniform, complained that, *"the britches were too big or too long."* It appears that all of the officers were well uniformed, most having acquired their uniforms from a seamstress or tailor, at their own expense. Most of the enlisted men had brought along their own bed rolls, which served them well since, like uniforms, government issued blankets were in short supply.

During Regiment's assignment to the Department of Middle and East Florida, Camp Davis, near Tallahassee, remained the main garrison headquarters, camp of instruction, and logistical base, for the First Florida Cavalry Regiment.

THE FIRST FLORIDA CAVALRY REGIMENT
CSA

★★★★★☐☐☐☐☐☐☐☐☐☐☐☐☐☐☐☐☐☐☐☐☐☐☐☐☐☐☐★★★★★

1861-62 Regimental Headquarters Staff

Colonel William George Mackey Davis--*Commanding Officer*
Lt. Colonel G. Troup Maxwell--*Executive Officer*
Major William Tennent Stockton--*Field Officer*
Captain William Footman--*Field Officer*
Dr. William Henry Pope--*Surgeon*
Dr. George P. Wilson..*Assistant Surgeon*
Elias E. Whitner--*Adjutant*
Sergeant-Major Thomas J. Shine--*Sergeant-Major*
Sgt. Thomas N. Footman--*Regimental Quartermaster Sergeant*
Sgt. James P. Harrison--*Regimental Commissary Sergeant*
Sgt. John F. Niblack-- *Regimental Ordinance Sergeant*

List Of The Regimental Sergeant-Majors
Thomas J. Shine 1861-July 1862
John Maxwell Footman July 1862-May 1863
Christie Gordon May 1863-July 1863
[NO ASSIGNED SERGEANT-MAJOR July 27 TO September 22, 1863]
Edmund Gillen September 23, 1863-April 1865

Regimental Musicians
Elbert E. Barker
John Falaney
William H. Futch
John Haws
Thomas Holton
William Howell [4]
Elijah Nix
Thomas Reese
Jonathan Roberts
Simeon A. Smith
Thomas Yarbour

7.

**********〇〇〇〇〇〇〇〇〇〇**********

BLACKSMITHS, TEAMSTERS, & FARRIERS

William Bryant, *Farrier*
William Coxe, *Teamster*
Abraham H. Colson, *Blacksmith*
Joseph Higgenbotham, *Farrier*
Elisha Carter, *Farrier-Teamster*
Benjamin L. Chandler, *Blacksmith*
Henry D. Berry, *Farrier*
Berian Dowling, *Farrier*
Jackson Smith, *Blacksmith*
James Brewer, *Farrier-Teamster*
David Hunter, *Blacksmith*
James Faulkner, *Blacksmith*
Stephen Godwin, *Farrier*
James Harrell, *Farrier-Teamster*
William H. Dinkins, *Blacksmith*
John W. Hines, *Blacksmith*
Jesse Curl Sr., *Farrier*
Owen W. Parker, *Blacksmith*
Monroe D. Hagin, *Farrier-Teamster*
William Ship, *Blacksmith-Teamster*
John W. Tanner, *Blacksmith*
William T. Adams, *Blacksmith*
James Miley, *Farrier-Teamster*

ORIGINAL COMPANY COMMANDERS AND FIRST SERGEANTS

COMPANY A
CAPTAIN ARTHUR ROBERTS
1ST SGT JOHN F. NIBLACK
COMPANY B
CAPTAIN JOHN G. HADDOCK
1ST SGT DRURY JONES
COMPANY C
CAPTAIN JOHN A. SUMMERLIN
1ST SGT WILLIAM WILSON
COMPANY D
CAPTAIN JOHN HARVEY
1ST SGT DARLING C. PRESCOTT
COMPANY E
CAPTAIN CHARLES F. CONE, Sr.
1ST SGT DAVID BELL
COMPANY F
CAPTAIN WILLIAM M. FOOTMAN
1ST SGT JOHN B. MacLEOD
COMPANY G
CAPTAIN WILLIAM D. CLARK
1ST SGT JAMES J. KENNARD
COMPANY H
CAPTAIN NOBLE A. HULL
1ST SGT MEREDITH E. BROCK
COMPANY I
CAPTAIN NICHOLAS S. COBB
1ST SGT THOMAS STARLING
COMPANY K
CAPTAIN DAVID HUGHES
1ST SGT ANDREW G. LaTASTE

8.

CHAPTER TWO

OPERATIONS IN FLORIDA

The Regiment's mission in northeast Florida was to reinforce defenses there, to reconnoiter the region, and to render forward protection for Jacksonville. Colonel W.G.M. Davis, in addition to commanding his regiment, spent a great deal of time on operational business for the Department of Middle and Eastern Florida. During his absence, Lt. Colonel George Troupe Maxwell assumed charge of the Regiment. George Maxwell had first enlisted at Monticello, as a private in the First Florida Infantry Regiment, and had briefly served as a company first sergeant before being discharged in July 1861. He then joined the First Cavalry where he received an appointment to lieutenant-colonel. Whenever Maxwell was absent, Major William Stockton, third in command, would take charge the Regiment. Major Stockton was the most experienced officer and was instrumental in training the Regiment in military tactics. The former West Point instructor wrote to his wife about, *"drilling 500 raw recruits whose officers know little and the men less,"* and then told how he was holding night school for the officers.

In mid-January 1862, the First Florida Cavalry's troop strength had reached 867 men, including 35 officers, of this total, 40 were absent, either sick, furloughed, or AWOL, and another 31 were reported on detached duty with other units or back at Camp Davis in Tallahassee. When the Regiment moved to East Florida, three companies, A, E, and F, under the charge of Captain William Footman, remained behind at Camp Davis. For a brief period, Footman continued instructing new recruits at Camp Davis while the main body of the Regiment began operations around Jacksonville. Out of necessity, the traditional "Camp of Instruction" was later abandoned and new enlistees were simply trained "on the job."

In East Florida, the Regiment was first stationed at Camp Trapier, near Callahan, along with several other Florida regiments, independent companies, and the 24th Mississippi Infantry Regiment. The First Cavalry camp was in a low area, which with the rain and winter cold, made for an especially harsh and unhealthy environment. Sanitation was deplorable, latrines were simple holes dug in the most convenient places, which often contaminated water sources. Ration issues were adequate, but the beef was of *"such poor quality that the men refused to eat it."* Subsistence usually consisted of desiccated potatoes, rice, salt pork, dried beans and hardtack. The troops often supplemented their rations by purchasing chickens and eggs from local civilians. Generally, coffee was plentiful as was sufficient issues of flour, corn meal, and lard. Biscuits and fried pork were among the most common food items prepared in the messes.

The confined quarters of camp life and the lack of sanitation promoted the spread of disease among the soldiers. Sickness began taking its toll among the troops in late January. Mumps, measles, and colds, ran rampant through the camps. Some of the men tried to treat themselves, or each other, the worst cases were dealt with by a surgeon of the 4th Florida

Infantry. By early February, nearly half of the 4th Florida Regiment was sick. Major Stockton reported that in one company of 70 men, 23 had the measles. It was reported that Colonel Davis, in spite of his reputation for strictness, was very compassionate when it came to his sick soldiers.

In the middle part of February, the Regiment held its first court martial. Serving as president of the court was Colonel Davis, with Major Stockton presiding as the judge advocate. The jury was made up of three officers from the Florida Special Battalion and three captains from the 24th Mississippi Regiment. The trial involved two officers, one from the First Florida Cavalry and the other from the Mississippi Regiment, both charged with drunkenness. While the case warranted minor disciplinary action, Colonel Davis no doubt welcomed the opportunity to set an example by which to encourage discipline in his command.

On February 18th, Secretary of War, J. P Benjamin, ordered the First Cavalry Regiment to move immediately to Tennessee and report to General Albert Sidney Johnston in Chattanooga. The Regiment would be mustered into Confederate service for the duration of the war and not just the 12 month enrollment as was expected by the men. Needless to say, this news was met with protests from the men. However, the Regiment was still lacking arms, equipment, and horses, and was certainly in no condition for such a move. Colonel Davis immediately left for Richmond to plead for Confederate support. Major Stockton was left in charge of the Regiment and Lt. Colonel Maxwell returned to Camp Davis to take care of garrison duties. Colonel Davis was still at odds with Governor Milton and probably desired that Maxwell stick close to Tallahassee. On February 22nd, Major Stockton ordered a mounted review of the First Cavalry Regiment at Camp Trapier. The Regiment had about 450 horses on duty in East Florida, and 250 at Camp Davis. Half of the horses in East Florida had already been determined to be in poor condition and unfit for service. This resulted in having to dismount three of the companies. All total, the Regiment had an estimated 900 mounts and wagon horses, or mules, of which only half were fit for service. Forage, feed, and good pasture grass, were scarce, and the quartermaster was without funds for maintaining the horses.

Meanwhile, the Federal forces, after successfully landing at Hilton Head, South Carolina, were now threatening Fernandina as Confederate troops at Fort Clinch, on the north end of Amelia Island, began preparations to pull back to the mainland. On February 27th, the Rebels began evacuating the island, leaving 15 guns behind at Fort Clinch. On the morning of March 2nd, a Union fleet under Flag Officer Samuel F. DuPont, appeared on the high seas east of Amelia Island. The expedition consisted of 26 ships, including 18 gunboats, along with a battalion of marines and one army brigade under Brigadier General Horatio Wright. The evacuation of Fernandina was accelerated by using trains to shuttle troops, goods, and civilians, over the river to the mainland. The trains were kept moving at Callahan Station with the help of Major Stockton and 25 First Cavalry soldiers, who quickly unloaded the arriving boxcars. The last evacuation train, crossing the trestle to the mainland, narrowly escaped damage when it was fired upon by a Union gunboat. On March 4th, Union forces made an unopposed landing at Fernandina and took control of

Amelia Island, which they would occupy until the end of the war. The First Florida Cavalry was assigned its first combat mission, to watch enemy movements and guard against intrusions into Confederate territory.

The First Florida Cavalrymen, realizing the seriousness of the situation in East Florida, became worried about their families back home. The enemy was presenting a real threat to the Florida homeland, yet the First Cavalrymen were under orders to leave their homes and families for Tennessee. Compounding their concerns was the fact that they had not been paid, nor given their promised horse allowances, and many were suffering with sickness. Now instead of 12 month enlistments, the War Department had extended the soldiers for the duration of the war. Morale was quickly deteriorating within the ranks. Disgruntled with their situation, the cavalrymen made it known that they would refuse orders to leave Florida. Several of the men had already deserted the Regiment and had returned to their homes. The Regiment was in a near state of mutiny. By March 16th, the troops were positively refusing to move until paid all back pay and allowances. In addition, they were demanding that a sufficient military force be left in Florida for the protection of their families. A paper was drawn up listing their grievances and demands. Several rank and file, including captains and lieutenants, signed and presented the document to Brigadier General Trapier. Fearing all out mutiny, General Trapier consulted with his superior, Major General J. C. Pemberton, commanding the Department of South Carolina. Pemberton directed Trapier to arrest and court martial all First Florida Cavalry officers who had signed the protest document. He further ordered General Trapier to read the Articles of War, numbers 7 and 8, to the entire First Florida Cavalry Regiment. [*Article 7 applied to officers or soldiers who incite mutiny. Article 8 had to do with soldiers who knowingly failed to take action to prevent mutiny. Both were court martial offenses carrying a maximum penalty of execution.*] General Trapier was further instructed to order the Regiment to prepare for movement to Tennessee. But in a letter, dated March 19th, Trapier notified the secretary of war, that *"owing to the limited means of transportation"* the First Cavalry had not commenced its transfer to Tennessee. Meanwhile, Colonel Davis, on his way back to Florida from Richmond, stopped to confer with General Pemberton about the mutinous state of the First Cavalry. Davis assured Pemberton that he could quell the situation without resulting to stronger means. But by the time Colonel Davis arrived in Florida, things had already calmed down. The Colonel then boarded the train for Tallahassee. He went to Camp Davis and proceeded to prepare the three mounted companies stationed there, to join the main body of the Regiment in their East Florida operations.

On March 23rd, at Callahan, six deserters were brought into the First Cavalry camp. Major Stockton ordered the deserters to be tied up and placed under guard. Later that evening, a group of local civilians showed up at Stockton's tent demanding that he release of the deserters. Major Stockton picked up his pistol, put on his sword, and called for the guard. Four guards with loaded rifles soon arrived at the scene. The major then stepped out of his tent and was confronted with about 24 local protestors. The men remained silent, but about a dozen women were quite vocal with their threats. One woman had two pistols and was carrying a double barreled shotgun. They demanded that the deserters be untied. Stockton refused and managed to quell the situation. As the crowd was leaving, one woman threatened, *"If these men are not untied, then murder will be committed tonight."* Some of the troops had gathered around to watch the excitement, until Stockton ordered, *"Men of the cavalry, unless you have business with me, go to your quarters."* Stockton turned around and was about to enter his tent when Sergeant John McLaughlin came up. McLaughlin, quartermaster sergeant for the 4th Infantry, informed the major of a rumor that the women were planning to throw an explosive shell into his tent that night. Stockton said that he doubted that they would carry out the plan, but would keep his six shooters handy just in case. The provost guard offered to post a sentinel at his tent, but Stockton refused the offer and added, *" my men will think I am afraid."* In quarters, behind Major Stockton's tent, lived his personal servant, named Sam. It was just before midnight when Stockton heard footsteps outside of his tent. He sprang to his door, threw back the flap and looked out, but only saw Sam sitting by the fire. Sam reported that someone had come by and was moving among the horses. The guard was called and a search was conducted but no one was found. Major Stockton returned to his quarters and had no more problems that night with the local civilians.

On the 24th, Colonel Davis arrived and ordered Major Stockton to move his seven companies closer to Jacksonville. The Confederates had evacuated the city leaving it under Federal occupation. Most of the Confederates had gathered at Baldwin, about 20 miles from Jacksonville. The next day at noon, Lt. Colonel Maxwell and Captain Footman arrived at Baldwin from Camp Davis with companies, A, E, and F. There was concern that the Federals might attempt an invasion into the interior of Florida. There were at least sixteen Yankee infantry companies inside Jacksonville and a number of other Federals surrounding the city. Stockton was ordered to take his companies and make a reconnaissance along each side of the railroad as far as Three Mile Creek west of the city. Some of the dismounted First Cavalry troops were temporarily attached as infantrymen to the Third Florida Infantry. Captain William Footman began operating to the south with his three mounted companies. Stockton's men reached Three Mile Creek without any sign of the enemy, but Captain Footman soon reported back that his horse troops had spotted a Union picket line positioned at the Brick Church in West La Villa, near Jacksonville. A detachment from the Third Florida Infantry, commanded by Lieutenant Thomas C. Strange, was deployed to attack the Union position. During the engagement four of the enemy were killed and three were taken prisoner. Lieutenant Strange suffered a mortal bullet wound and died the next day. Although the Rebels suffered one death and a few minor wounds in their first serious engagement, they were victorious in forcing the Federals to fall back into the city of Jacksonville.

Following the raid at the Brick Church, three mounted companies of the First Florida Cavalry Regiment, under Footman, remained on patrol duty west of Jacksonville keeping watch over the enemy. Company K, under Captain Hughes, was posted to guard a bridge on the road between

Baldwin and Jacksonville. The other companies, for the time being, were camped near the intersection of the Florida Railroad and the Florida, Atlantic, and Gulf Central Railroad. The Regiment's mission was soon changed when the War Department issued the following special orders to the headquarters of the Department of East and Middle Florida.

Special Order No. 118.
Dept. East and Middle Florida
Colonel Davis with the First Florida Cavalry will proceed to Camp Langford with his whole command and relieve Colonel Dilsworth and the 3rd Regiment Florida Volunteers, provided Colonel Hopkins' 4th Regiment of Volunteers is not present. As soon as the arms now enroute for Lake City shall have arrived at that point Colonel Davis with his regiment will proceed immediately to Tennessee and report to General A.S. Johnston.

Following the operations around Jacksonville, and in compliance with the above order, the First Cavalry Regiment transferred to Camp Langford, on the mainland across from Amelia Island. Their mission was to prevent the enemy from leaving the island and penetrating the Confederate line into Florida's interior. They were to watch all enemy movements and report any useful intelligence to headquarters. Camp Langford was a primitive camp situated on a bluff, close to water, and sheltered from view by thick woods and palmetto bushes. Each company had a row of quarters, a combination of palmetto huts and government issued shelter halves. The horses were tied to a line in front of the shelters. The forage, although still scarce, was stored between the quarters and at the end of each row of shelters was a designated mess area for cooking. The teamsters, farriers, and wagons were placed in the rear of the quarters area. Beyond this were the latrines, or "sinks." At the head of the companies were the staff quarters and the surgeon's tent. For the most part, the camp layout basically conformed to the regulation book for cavalry bivouacs.

Companies "G" and "H" were assigned to the north sector of the St. Marys River while "F" company patrolled the railroad leading from Amelia Island. Companies "I" and "K" were assigned to watch the sector south of the railroad. At least three other companies, of dismounted troops, were assigned to picket duty, the provost guard, or building defensive earthworks. A small detachment, of 30 to 60 men, was still in Leon County, at Camp Davis, probably for logistical purposes.

The first recorded engagement occured when Company "G," commanded by Captain Clark, was ordered to take up a position on a high bluff overlooking the St. Marys River. It was expected that the Federals would try testing the Rebel lines by sending an expedition up the river. On this occasion, Captain Clark spotted an enemy gunboat approaching from Cumberland Sound. As the vessel drew closer, a lookout perched on the masthead caught a glimpse of Clark's company concealed in the palmettos and yelled to his shipmates, *"There's the damn Rebels!"* Having been spotted, Captain Clark raised his rifle and fired a single shot hitting the lookout, the man fell to the deck. The rest of the company began firing as the Yankee gunboat swiftly turned around and withdrew to a safe distance.

The Regiment was still in bad need of arms and ammunition. Many of the men were furnishing their own rifles, or shotguns, and some had no weapons at all. The shortage of weapons may have been one reason why some soldiers remained at Camp Davis. But on March 22nd, a blockade runner had made it into Mosquito Inlet with 9000 arms. A Third Infantry company, stationed at New Smyrna, was ordered to unload and ship the guns to Richmond for distribution to the Confederate army. While in shipment on the railroad near Callahan, a large number of these rifles was "procured" by the 7th Florida Infantry, the First Florida Cavalry, and several independent companies. Desperate for arms, and with Governor Milton's *"unauthorized approval,"* Colonel Davis acquired and issued 180 of the rifles to his First Cavalrymen. This led to an investigation by the Confederate War Department to reclaim the weapons. [*However by the time the inquiry had been completed, the First Cavalry Regiment was out of state and, apparently, allowed to retain the subject weapons*].

In early April, Colonel Davis, in preparation for the march to Tennessee, inspected the Regiment's horses and found them to be in a serious state. The lack of forage, hard use, and severe weather, had rendered most of the horses unfit for service. *"Two hundred of them,"* reported Davis, *"should be condemned or put in some wild pasture."* He suggested that two thirds of the horses, *"...ought to be sent to Payne's Prairie and put to pasture."* A number of the Regiment's horses had died and others had gone lame on marches and were simply abandoned. Davis admitted that the Regiment was unfit to proceed as a cavalry, unless the government would be willing to furnish new horses in Tennessee. *"The horses as they are,"* noted Colonel Davis, *"would not be worth what it would cost the government to feed them on the road and the pay allowed for their use."* The First Cavalry still had 250 good horses at Camp Davis and about the same number of fit mounts in East Florida. One infantry soldier, upon seeing the horses, wrote, *"Half their horses are broken down with ribs poking out & not fit to mount."* The way it looked, the Regiment would lack 400 mounts when it came time to leave for Tennessee. Another problem was that some of the men, in order to join the cavalry, had purchased their horses on credit with their officers standing good for payment. Concerned with this fact, Colonel Davis remarked, *"I do not recommend condemnation of the horses unless some compensation is made to the men."* In early April, the First Florida Cavalry troops were pacified somewhat when they received back pay, but the record is not clear as to whether, or not, they were paid their overdue horse allowances.

Sickness continued to haunt the First Florida Cavalry soldiers with the most severe cases involving measles or mumps. Private John Garner, of Co. I, caught the measles and was sent by train to the Lake City hospital where he died on April 8th, 1862. Private Garner may have been the Regiment's first recorded fatality. The next afternoon, another cavalryman, Private Burrell Mobley, of Co. F, succumbed to an unspecified illness.

On April 7th, a Union soldier, Private William W. Lunt of the 9th Maine Infantry, fell into the custody of a First Cavalry picket. Private Lunt was captured on the mainland while walking along the railroad from Amelia Island. Private Lunt was escorted under guard to Camp Langford and interrogated by Colonel Davis. Supposedly, Lunt had robbed a woman he had met while walking along the railroad tracks. The woman was Ellen Manning, who also went by the nickname *"Big Ellen."* She had authorized passage to and from Fernandina and may have been engaged in spy work for Colonel Davis. Records indicate that the women on Amelia Island had a discreet system of signals by which they communicated with people on the mainland. In one correspondence, believed written by Colonel Davis, reference is made to, *"...the assistance by parties of civilians"* in watching enemy movements. Naturally any spy agents would have been confidential, but Ellen Manning's known activities certainly raises speculation that she may have been a Confederate informant. Big Ellen frequently visited various Rebel camps and often visited the O'Neil house at the head of the trestle to Amelia Island, a known "gathering spot" for Union soldiers. The house, owned by a Judge O'Neil, who had evacuated, was lived in by Catherine Heath. Mrs. Heath's husband had been held under arrest on Amelia Island by the Federals since their landing at Fernandina. Big Ellen often visited on the island with passes signed by Colonel Davis. Ellen certainly had close observation of the enemy. She may have played Private Lunt into his capture by the First Cavalry, or perhaps Lunt may have been a Union deserter. Whatever the case, William Lunt's ordeal, and Ellen Manning's role, remains a mystery still pondered by local historians.

The Federals began evacuating Jacksonville on April 9th. Colonel Davis, on three occasions, met with Union General Horatio G. Wright concerning the safety of Jacksonville residents. It was feared that renegade bands of Florida refugees might return and seek revenge against those who had remained in Jacksonville during the Union occupation. Colonel Davis moved in a small force of dismounted cavalry and infantry for insuring the safety of the residents. It should be noted that the Confederates never maintained a regular occupation in Jacksonville. In the later stages of the war, the city would again be occupied by Federal forces.

On April 10th, Company F captured two Union soldiers pumping a handcar down the railroad line near the O'Neil house. Following this capture, Captain Footman lead his 40 man company in an attack against a Union guard posted at the O'Neil house. Curiously enough, Catherine Heath was not at home at the time of the attack, perhaps she had been forewarned by the Confederates. In the engagement Captain Footman's cavalry captured the following Union soldiers; Sergeant Richard Weaver, Corporal James Bowman, along with Privates Isaac Whitney, John E. Kent, Alonzo B. Merill, and Wesley Adams. During the assault, Union Private Ansel Chase was killed. The prisoners were gathered up and sent by train to Tallahassee.

Colonel Davis, in a rather unusual move on April 10th, turned Private Lunt over to the Federals aboard the U.S.S. Ottawa. Why Lunt was not sent with the other prisoners raises questions, but in a communiqué to Union Colonel Bisbee, commanding the 9th Maine at Fernandina, Davis accused Lunt of robbery and assault on Ellen Manning. Colonel Bisbee in turn brought charges against William Lunt for desertion and giving information to the Rebels which resulted in the attack on the Union outpost at the O'Neil house. The evidence was circumstantial, but enough to court martial Private Lunt. The trial, held in St. Augustine, found Lunt guilty of all charges. William Lunt was only 21 years old when he was executed by a firing squad December 1, 1862, at Hilton Head Island. His remains are in an unmarked grave in the Beaufort National Cemetery.

Following Footman's attack at the O'Neil house, his Company "F" was increased to 100 men and along with Company "G," continued to operate from Camp Langford. Major Stockton was ordered to remove the other companies from Langford to Camp Trapier.

Soon after arriving at Camp Trapier several soldiers fell to sickness and one man died in Company "B." General Trapier requested another delay in the Regiment's movement to Tennessee due to the condition of the horses and sickness among the troops. Colonel Davis blamed the condition of his horses and men on exposure to the weather and the government's failure to provide for their needs. He was then ordered to remove the Regiment from East Florida and assemble it at Camp Davis. The Regiment packed up and began moving back to Tallahassee.

At Camp Davis, a decision was made to dismount the Regiment. In spite of several political attempts to convert the entire First Cavalry to infantry, Davis argued in favor of keeping part of the unit mounted and retaining the designation of *Cavalry*. Davis believed that his men were well trained in cavalry tactics and anticipated that the government would remount the Regiment once it was in Tennessee. A decision was made to keep three companies, A, E, and F, mounted as a squadron under Captain William Footman. The other seven companies dismounted on May 13th to serve as foot soldiers. The Regiment was redesignated the First Florida Cavalry Regiment *Dismounted*. Many of the poor horses were sent to pasture on Payne's Prairie, some were transferred to other units, a few were destroyed, and others were herded back to the homes of the soldiers. According to the account of Private William C. Hawkins, his horse was among those in "K" Company that were driven back to Hillsborough County from Jacksonville by Captain Hughes' Black servant. This may indicate that some of the companies, or soldiers with privately owned horses, may have dismounted before leaving East Florida for Camp Davis.

In the early morning hours of May 8th, Lt. Colonel Maxwell headed Footman's three mounted companies out of Camp Davis on the long journey to Tennessee. The dismounted companies moved by rail to Madison to prepare for their northward march through Georgia. A few men from "B" and "D" companies remained mounted to accompany the wagon train. Major Stockton departed from his home at Quincy to head the dismounted companies. He traveled in advance to take care of any required logistics during the movement. Colonel Davis became ill and could not leave with his command until later.

The Regiment made the march in three separate groups. The mounted squadron was headed by Lt. Colonel Maxwell on a route from Tallahassee through Albany, Buena Vista, and Talbotton, to Cartersville, Georgia. Major William Stockton's dismounted companies, B, C, D, G, H, I, and K, marched to Quitman, Georgia, then to Albany. This same route was followed by the Regiment's wagon train, which picked up any stragglers or sick troopers. Many of the sick, too weak to travel, were left scattered in private homes along the way.

The journey was a combination of horseback, railroad, and long foot marches over dusty clay roads. In the eyes of these Floridians, Georgia was a foreign land, gone were the palmetto trees and moss drenched live oaks so familiar to Floridians. They were flatlanders, not use to marching over hills, but the rolling clay hills of Georgia were nothing compared to the mountains they would soon face in Tennessee. The march was weary and filled with varying degrees of homesickness, but their spirits were bolstered by cheers as they paraded through the small Georgia towns. *"Seeing the flags & young ladys coming out of homes to wave & cheer us kept us on the march,"* wrote Private Braddock of "B" company.

On May 19th, Major Stockton made arrangements at Macon to transport the dismounted troops by train from Macon to Atlanta. It is not certain, but the dismounted troops may have traveled by train from Albany to Macon. Major Stockton kept in communication throughout the movement with Lt. Colonel Maxwell and Colonel Davis. According to Stockton, the three mounted companies were without their captains and half of their lieutenants during the march. It is not known if Captain Footman was with the squadron, however Lt. Colonel Maxwell appears to have been in charge of the mounted companies during most of the march. The three mounted companies reached Cartersville, Georgia, on May 24th and set up camp to await the arrival of the dismounted companies. In the meantime, the horses were taken 16 miles northeast of Cartersville for forage and rest. On May 26th, the dismounted companies arrived by train from Atlanta, followed shortly after by the wagon train. The wagons, noted Major Stockton, were loaded with the sick and lame on board. *"I was proud of my command as they marched steadily through this place."* wrote Stockton to his wife, *"Not one sound from them except the tramp of the hoofs of horses and the wagons of the command. I had told the commanding officers to break by fours and keep the men closed, of course I was the observed, being in full uniform, sword & etc."*

One man was left behind in Cartersville with the mumps and, according to Major Stockton, the sick man was properly cared for at the home of the Jones family. *"I have just been out to see the sick man."* wrote Stockton, *"He is far better, he is in a good room,... the south room of the house."*

On the journey from Florida, at least ten First Cavalry soldiers died of sickness, another ten were given disability discharges, several were left in an Atlanta hospital, many others were left sick in towns along the march, and more than ten had deserted. The First Cavalry personnel strength had dropped by about 200 men since leaving East Florida.

In late May 1862, the Regiment held elections, which changed much of the leadership at company level. Captain Nicholas Cobb, commander of Company I, was replaced by Henry Bradford. Lieutenant Joseph F. Pons was elected captain of D Company and Stephen Weeks replaced Captain William D. Clark of G Company. A significant number of lieutenants either resigned or were not reelected. Several non-commissioned officers were promoted to lieutenant. Captain William Footman, of Company F, commander of the three companies designated as the mounted squadron, unofficially took the title of "acting major." There is no indication that Footman, while with the First Florida Cavalry, was ever officially promoted to the rank of major, although he often used it socially and in signing papers, and certainly carried the responsibility of a major. Respectfully, Footman will be referred to as "major" in this history.

The First Florida Cavalry companies reunited as a regiment in Bartow County, Georgia, to begin their final 75 mile march to Tennessee. Major Footman's mounted squadron led the advance, followed by the dismounted companies and the supply wagons. Colonel William Davis, now recovered from his brief illness, had left Tallahassee and was enroute by train to rejoin his Regiment in Tennessee. Upon arriving in Tennessee, the First Florida Cavalry Regiment established its headquarters at Shellmound, about 26 miles south of Chattanooga. Here it was officially assigned to Leadbetter's Brigade under the Department of East Tennessee, commanded by former West Point professor, Major-General Edmund Kirby Smith, a Florida born veteran of the Mexican War and several Indian wars. General Smith, as a previous United States officer, had commanded cavalry out West, and the fact that he was a Floridia native, caused optimism among the dismounted companies that he would surely remount the First Florida Cavalry on government horses. For a brief period, the expectation of getting horses bolstered spirits of the 1st Cavalrymen. In the meantime, they were willing to serve a short time as foot soldiers while proudly emphasizing their designation of "dismounted cavalry." As one Florida cavalryman reportedly argued to a Georgia infantry sergeant, *"Dismounted cavalry just means we're waiting on fresh horses, 'cause we rode the old ones to the ground."*

CHAPTER THREE

FROM TENNESSEE TO KENTUCKY

On June 3, 1862, the dismounted companies were ordered to cross the Tennessee River and proceed northwest of Chattanooga to Winchester. They were to join with forces supporting Colonel John Adam's brigade, however, before reaching Winchester, they were redirected to hold a mountain pass between Chattanooga and Bridgeport, Alabama.

Chattanooga, nestled between high mountain ridges, was a main portal between the North and the South. Federal forces, under General Buell, were threatening to gain control of this strategic point. The Confederates were determined to defend this doorway to the South and were unwilling to give an inch to Buell's Yankees. General Braxton Bragg, bent on denying Buell's army any opportunities, began racing his Rebel troops toward Chattanooga. The First Florida Cavalry soldiers soon found themselves as players in this risky contest and served several roles as defenders holding the Southern lines around Chattanooga.

The hopes of remounting the full regiment soon faded away for the lack of available horses. The Confederate army needed all the horses it could muster for pulling wagons and artillery, and could not afford the hundreds that would be required to mount a full cavalry regiment. However, Companies A, E, and F, of the First Florida Cavalry would remain mounted as a detached squadron.

Major William Footman was ordered to take his mounted squadron and keep watch along the Tennessee River. The Squadron carried along a blacksmith wagon and two wagons of fodder and feed. Footman's cavalrymen operated company size patrols from a small camp on the banks of the Tennessee west of Chattanooga.

Prior to June 12th, the dismounted portion of the Regiment was subjected to a full day of concentrated shelling from Federal guns. This was probably the first heavy engagement for the First Florida Cavalry, but in defiance of intense enemy fire, they held their ground and suffered no reported casualties.

On June 13th, Colonel William G. M. Davis learned that the Federals were crossing the river just south of the Regiment's position. Major William Stockton immediately deployed 350 dismounted troops to previously prepared trench works to protect the Regiment's rear flanks. Soon, these dismounted men were engaged in a series of light skirmishes that went on for nearly a week until the enemy pulled out. On June 18th, a detachment of dismounted First Florida Cavalrymen was sent across to the north side of the Tennessee River where they attacked a minor enemy force. Four bluecoats were killed and several others were captured. The next day an estimated 4000 Yankees, in a show of force, advanced within five miles of the Rebel line. The Florida Cavalry, combined with other regiments of their brigade, prepared for what they expected to be a big battle. The Confederates were ordered to cross the river and meet the enemy. Relying on a limited number of flatboats, the only troops who

19.

successfully crossed the river were about 320 dismounted soldiers of the First Florida Cavalry Regiment. After reaching the other side, these troops pushed forward with an objective of blocking a mountain pass, but instead found themselves facing a small Union cavalry. A firing contest quickly erupted, which was fierce, but of short duration. The Floridians claimed the victory with the Federals loosing six men, including two officers, and two horses. Several other Yankees were wounded and four were taken prisoner. The Floridians suffered only minor wounds. Major William Stockton, who had led the expedition, reported that the enemy, "...*were nearly all Germans, calling themselves the Kentucky Cavalry.*"

By the 21st, the Regiment was standing guard at the narrows of the Tennessee, about five miles south of Whitesides. The dismounted Florida Cavalry, along with other regiments, seemed to change camps almost daily. In late June, the Floridians pulled back to Lookout Mountain to drill and for a brief rest. Footman's mounted Floridians continued scouting for the brigade, often at great distances from the main Regiment. In early July, Colonel Davis ordered the Regiment to relocate to Grantham Station, about 27 miles south of Chattanooga. On July 4th, the dismounted companies were involved in a fight against the 37th Indiana Infantry. The First Cavalry only suffered a horse killed, but managed to capture a Union major. That night the captured officer shared the hospitality of Major Stockton's tent. A temporary cease fire was called between the 37th Indiana and the 1st Florida Cavalry, to allow a meeting of commanders from both sides. On the banks of the Tennessee, Lt. Colonel Maxwell and Major Stockton, with Sergeant-Major Shine, met with the adjutant from the 37th Indiana. The adjutant had brought over the captured major's baggage. Maxwell, Stockton, and the Union officer had a long and strangely pleasant conversation. The adjutant told the Florida officers that his troops were tired of war, but were confident that the South would be conquered. After this friendly encounter, the officers shook hands, saluted, and returned to their respective sides to become enemies once more.

The next day, train loads of Confederate troops began arriving in and around Chattanooga. Rumors began circulating that something was about to happen. The next night, Colonel Perry's [the former Florida governor] Seventh Florida Infantry Regiment joined the First Cavalry's camp at Grantham Station. This was a welcomed reunion since many of the soldiers of these two units were from the same families. Private William Hawkins of the 1st Florida Cavalry met up with one of his kin, First Sergeant Daniel Hawkins of the 7th Florida Infantry. They had not seen each other since leaving home back in Manatee County. All of the men were eager to exchange news from home and swap a little gossip. For the few men who could read or write, writing materials were scarce. However, mail did flow regularly between Florida and the regiments; although it often took a month for a letter to reach a soldier. Most of the enlisted soldiers received little, or no mail, and frequently relied on verbal news that passed through the ranks from one soldier to another.

The First Florida Cavalry, on June 30th, was garrisoned as part of the Post of Chattanooga, but within a week, Colonel Davis assumed command of the second brigade in General Heth's division of the Army of East

Tennessee. Davis' brigade included the First Florida Cavalry Regiment, the 6th and 7th Florida Infantry Regiments, and the Marion Artillery Battery. Davis moved his brigade back to Grantham Station, *"where the water was so bad that the men had to dig shallow wells."* The July heat had parched their mouths so much, that the soldiers had little option but to drink from this only available water source.

There was a shortage of officers in the 1st Florida Cavalry at this time, mostly due to resignations and lack of new appointments. Major Stockton complained that, *"Things are not working smoothly for want of a military system. Nobody knows who are officers and who are not."* Colonel Davis was trying to supervise both the Regiment and the Brigade. Stockton, being a West Point man gave his opinion and said that he would rather see Davis in charge of only the Regiment. In Stockton's opinion the Regiment should be divided into two wings, with himself in command of the left wing and Maxwell in charge of the right, and Davis as the central commander.

Meanwhile, back in Florida, Governor Milton was busy penning another letter to the secretary of war complaining that Florida had been left without adequate defenses. He placed the blame on the Confederacy for ordering so many regiments from the state. In the letter, Milton claimed that many cavalry officers had resigned and returned to Florida after being denied the right to elections of their field officers. As usual, the governor found an opportunity to rant about Colonel Davis. *"Without an election,"* wrote Milton, *"...and therefore without proper legal authority, Colonel William G. M. Davis is in command of the [2nd Brigade] and claiming to rank by seniority Colonel Finley, of the 6th Regiment, Colonel Perry, of the 7th Regiment, and Colonel Dilsworth, of the 3rd Regiment, which is considered unjust to these officers and their regiments, as well as to the First Florida Cavalry Regiment."* However, most records indicate that William G. M. Davis held seniority by date of rank. Having grown use to the governor's criticism and complaining, there was no official response.

Since arriving in Tennessee, six First Cavalry soldiers had died of disease, yet only one, at this point in time, is known to have been seriously wounded in combat. Sickness constantly plagued the Regiment and kept its fighting strength reduced by significant numbers.

Command of the Regiment was turned over to Lt. Colonel George Maxwell and for a brief period the Florida soldiers were stationed at Camp Hill, 30 miles below Chattanooga. On July 17th, Abraham Colson was promoted to blacksmith and Joseph Higgenbottom was made farrier. A few new officers were elected and Major Stockton was sent to Knoxville to recruit replacements for the Regiment. Soon the Regiment was ordered to Loudon as part of Davis' Brigade. On the 27th, Colonel Davis was directed to turn his brigade over to Colonel Perry and to report to Knoxville, where he temporarily assumed command of the Post at Knoxville. Meanwhile in Chattanooga, Generals Braxton Bragg and Kirby Smith, were planning a cooperative invasion into Kentucky. The Kentuckian loyalty was still split between the North and the South. Bragg was of the opinion that if he could rid the bluegrass of Yankees, then the citizens could be swayed to the Southern side. A plan was drawn up to invade Kentucky using three columns. Bragg's army would push up through middle Tennessee into the heart of Kentucky. Kirby Smith would head his center column north into Lexington with Humphrey Marshall's troops on the right wing. As an added measure, John Morgan's 900 man heavy cavalry would cover the outer fringes of the invasion and attack the enemy's weak points.

By August 4th, the 1st Cavalry Regiment had assembled with its brigade at Knoxville. Two days later, orders came down, *"have 3 days rations prepared and to hold in readiness to move out at a moments warning."* Northeast of Knoxville, a Confederate force, under Stevenson, had engaged the enemy at Tazwell and was driving them back to Cumberland Gap. The 1st Cavalry was all set to move as reinforcements until General Stevenson telegraphed that he *"didn't need any help."* The Post of Knoxville became a staging area for Kirby Smith's invasion force as reinforcements began arriving by rail from Chattanooga. The troops had no knowledge of the invasion plans, but it was obvious that a major campaign was about to be launched. In preparation for the march, the 1st Cavalry discharged several of its men for disabilities. John Wright, 50 years old, became lame and could no longer take the long marches. James Dowling, who had enlisted as a substitute for R. B. Davis, was discharged. The three Roziers, Charles R., Charles H, and Soloman, all of Company C, took discharges under the conscript law and set out for Florida. Major Footman's mounted squadron was detached from the Regiment to ride with Colonel John S. Scott's heavy cavalry. The Florida squadron, on August 13th, rode out of Knoxville and headed for Clinton as part of the advance guard. Major Stockton would ride with Footman's troops into Kentucky and Lt. Colonel Maxwell would take charge of the dismounted companies of the Regiment. The main body of Kirby Smith's invasion force pulled out of Knoxville early the next morning, made up of four brigades, including Davis' Brigade of Florida regiments serving under General Heth's division. Colonel Davis moved his brigade through Big Creek Gap and into Barbourville, Kentucky. The Rebels passed to the west of the Union at Cumberland Gap, however, Kirby Smith, concerned about 8000 Yankees there, positioned a division to block any offensive move by the Federals.

The Florida soldiers found the rugged mountainous terrain of Kentucky especially difficult. Crossing the mountains was an overwhelming task and caused the wagons to lag a week behind the troops. It took the teamsters a full day and night, to get all the wagons over the mountains. In some places block and tackle was used to assist the mules in pulling the wagons over rocks. They were constantly harassed by bushwhacking Union loyalists, which they called "Jayhawkers." One 1st Cavalry soldier wrote, *"They just pop up from behind a rock and shoot us & begone fore we could shoot back."* One dismounted company from the First Florida Cavalry, was detailed to guard the brigade wagon train against bushwhackers.

The Confederate expedition reached Barbourville on August 18th, where they regrouped and rested for a week. The 6th and 7th Florida Regiments, along with the Marion Artillery and its three field guns, were sent to secure positions at Williamsburg. Footman's squadron, with the advance cavalry force, had pushed ahead to the Rockcastle River and had secured a fording place for the invasion force.

To the West, Braxton Bragg was aiming his 27,000 Confederates in the direction of Louisville. General Buell, working almost parallel to Bragg, was driving his Yankee forces northward in a race to stay ahead of the invaders. However, Braxton Bragg, after capturing Munfordville, diverted his army away from Louisville to link up with Kirby Smith's Confederates at Frankfort. Unfortunately this allowed General Buell to seize Louisville and refresh his Federal army; ultimately this would cost the Confederates the campaign. But Bragg wasn't focused on Louisville, he was planning to install a Confederate governor in the Kentucky capital at Frankfort.

Kirby Smith's forces pulled out of Barbourville on the 25th and headed for London, Kentucky. From a distance, the Rebel invaders looked like a formidable force, but up close the soldiers were a dusty, ragged, and half starved lot. Their route was scattered with the sick and lame all the way back to the Tennessee border. Many of the sick were organized into squads and sent walking back to Tennessee. These squads often fell into enemy hands. One such squad of First Florida Cavalry men, consisting of John Johns, Absolam Townsend, William Scarbourough, and Andrew Varnes, was captured at Pine Mountain. At Barbourville, First Cavalry privates Kinchen Bell and Hiram Beasley were left behind, too sick to make the march. Private Baxter Leach, of Company H, was left sick on the banks of the Rockcastle River and was never heard from again.

Provisions were desperately lacking due to the supply wagons being so far behind the troops. Soldiers resorted to living off the land along the march, raiding apple orchards and corn fields, and even begging for handouts as they passed by farm houses. At Barbourville, the Rebels had found a salt deposit, almost every soldier had procured a pocket full, or small sack of salt, which helped to enhance the rather dull diet of apples and roasting ears. The troops joked that *"C.S.A."* stood for *"Corn, Salt, and Apples."* But the salt also brought a thirst that was not too easily quenched, especially since a drought had made water as scarce as rations. *"They wuz spiting cotton & choking on dust & praying for rain all the way to Richmond"* wrote a Kentuckian observer of the march.

By the afternoon of August 29th, the Confederate army had reached the crest of Big Hill, between Kingston and Richmond. Colonel Scott's cavalry, the eyes and ears of Kirby Smith's force, reported that the Union army had drawn a line across the Rebel's path. These were General Nelson's Kentuckian bluecoats, made up mostly of green recruits, some with less than a week in service. Still they presented an obstacle which had to be dealt with. The Southern troops had been steady on the march since leaving London and were hungry, thirsty, and well worn down. In spite of these conditions, Kirby Smith decided upon an immediate attack, believing that a bold stand would lead to a quick victory. The long Confederate column was halted as the senior officers surveyed the problem and planned their attack strategy. The next day, General Smith learned that the Yankees had moved up on a line five miles south of Richmond. General Cleburne's Confederates would be the first to challenge the enemy. After a brief brush with Cleburne's forces, the Federals began retreating into the town of Richmond. Both sides began positioning for the Battle of Richmond. The First Florida Cavalry mounted squadron, led by William Footman, performed gallantly in several charges against the enemy at Mount Zion Church and at White's Farm. The Battle of Richmond ended in an overwhelming victory for the Rebels. Kirby Smith's army used about 5000 Southern troops against the enemy, capturing 4303 prisoners and a complete U.S. wagon train. The Rebels lost only 78 killed and 372 wounded, compared to Union casualties of 206 killed and 844 wounded. The dismounted companies of the First Florida Cavalry Regiment arrived a day later and were not engaged at Richmond. The day after the battle was Sunday, General Smith ordered all of the regiments to assemble with their chaplains to give thanks for the victory at Richmond. The remainder of the day was spent on burial details and caring for the wounded. Major Footman's First Cavalry squadron had moved on north of Richmond to keep watch over the retreating Yankees.

Heth's 2nd Division, including Colonel Davis heading the 6th Brigade, moved in to occupy Richmond. Colonel Maxwell was absent on administrative duty and had not yet caught up with the Regiment. Major Stockton was in charge of the 1st Florida Cavalry's dismounted companies at Richmond. Colonel Davis, no longer commanding the Regiment, was now serving as a brigade commander. Colonel Maxwell was the Regiment's commander, with Major Stockton as second in command, while Major Footman remained in charge of the mounted companies. General E. Kirby Smith's army, while technically still under the Department of East Tennessee, was renamed "The Army of Kentucky."

On September 1st, the Confederates moved across the Kentucky River and had made camp *"within a rebel yell of Lexington."* Footman's squadron had returned late that evening for supplies and was camped with the First Cavalry Regiment. That night, Lexington citizens could see the glows from thousands of Rebel campfires sprinkled across the rolling landscape. Earlier that evening, General Smith had called a meeting of his division commanders to plan their entrance into Lexington. No one was expecting any resistance, but Kirby Smith wanted to make sure that his troops would make a favorable impression on the citizenry. One sergeant remarked, *"We was told to march straight and behave or else the colonel would be on our backsides."*

The next morning, the Confederates entered Lexington like a grand parade, although considerably dusty and well worn. With battle flags flying, General Kirby Smith, and his staff, led the long grey column of Southern soldiers into the town. The headquarters entourage was followed by several hundred mounts of heavy cavalry, which were strung out for nearly a mile, while light cavalry patrolled the outskirts of the town for security. Local civilians gathered to watch as the cavalry filed past followed by divisions of infantry being trailed by rumbling artillery pieces and a wagon train that stretched beyond the hills. Major Stockton described the event in a letter, *"[We were] welcomed with cheers, with smiles, with tears of joy. Never have I witnessed such ovation, Confederate flags were flying from every window."* For the First Florida Cavalrymen, it was a brief moment of glory and they held their heads high, like conquerors, as they marched proudly through the streets of Lexington.

Lexington, Kentucky, now belonged to Kirby Smith's Confederates, but the long march had been costly in terms of sickness and scarcity of supplies. Major Footman arrived with his squadron and submitted a request to the quartermaster for clothing. Sickness had taken its share of Footman's Floridians leaving a number of vacant saddles. In order to replace his sick cavalrymen, Footman began recruiting from the First Florida's dismounted companies. Sergeant John Lloyd, of Company B, was remounted to ride with Footman's squadron, and no doubt, was glad to transfer from foot to horseback. John Wesley Hines replaced David Hunter as blacksmith for the mounted squadron.

The First Florida Cavalry troops did not remain in Lexington for long. Colonel Davis was ordered to proceed with his brigade, which included the First Florida Cavalry, the 6th and 7th Florida Infantry regiments, to the Kentucky capital of Frankfort. The mounted squadron led the advance making sure the route was clear of any Union opposition. The 1st Florida Cavalry dismounted companies, on September 1st, were among the first regiments to reach Frankfort.

The ranks of the Florida Cavalry were being thinned out by sickness, with more than half of its soldiers suffering from chronic diarrhea, pneumonia, malnourishment, mumps, and typhoid fever. Hospitals in Lexington and Frankfort were filled more with diseased soldiers than with battle casualties. Many of the Florida soldiers found care in private homes. In Frankfort, Mrs. Arabella Montgomery had taken in several ill troopers from the 1st Cavalry, the 6th and 7th Florida Infantry Regiments.

On September 4th, a composite unit, consisting of some First Florida Cavalry dismounted companies, and other troops, under Heth's division, went north on a expedition to the Ohio River. After two days of hard marching, these troops reached a point on the river across from Covington, Ohio. Historically, this was the northernmost point reached by elements of the First Florida Cavalry Regiment during the Civil War.

Not all of the First Cavalry troops made it to the Ohio River, some were retained in reserve at Frankfort. This reserve portion of the 1st Cavalry was ordered to proceed to Lebanon, by way of the ford at McCown's ferry near Springfield, to attack a small enemy force. The order stressed, *"The General wishes especially that* [the commands] *shall behave in an orderly manner during the march, otherwise the people cannot be favorably impressed."* Once again, General Kirby Smith seemed as much focused on winning the loyalty of the Kentuckians as he was on throwing out the Yankee army. Details of the Lebanon operation are not known, however, within two days, these men had returned to Frankfort.

On September 10th, after being briefly split up in several directions, most of the Florida regiments were back in Lexington. The next day, Major Footman rode into Lexington and picked up 480 pounds of corn and 560 pounds of hay for his mounted squadron. The requisition form stated that this supply was for one days ration for 40 horses. The estimated personnel strength of Footman's three mounted companies at this time, if based on supply requisitions, was less than 100 able men, including the farriers.

Footman's squadron spent most of the Kentucky campaign on detached duty and was seldom with the 1st Florida Cavalry dismounted companies. The mounted squadron was usually employed on long range patrols and in risky guerrilla operations. On September 21st, while patrolling north of Frankfort, in Henry County, the squadron was attacked by an enemy force at New Castle. The encounter, which is described as an ambush in official records, was quick and fierce. During the engagement, Private Irving Kinard broke his leg when he fell from his horse and Private Lewis Davis was wounded and his horse was killed. Both Thomas Davis and William A. J. Howard were killed during the attack. In the confusion of battle, Lewis Davis was left behind for dead, however, he survived and managed to hide out for a month until he was captured by the Yankees.

Meanwhile, to the southwest, Braxton Bragg had concentrated his Confederate corps at Bardstown. Bragg's, and Smith's, Confederate forces, about forty thousand in number, were scattered along a 60 mile line from Bardstown up to Lexington. At the same time, in Louisville, the two Union generals, Buell and Nelson, were reorganizing their U. S. forces for an offensive against the invading Rebels.

In Frankfort, Colonel Davis had assumed command of about a thousand troops concentrated there, including the First Florida Cavalry's dismounted companies. The effective fighting strength of Davis' command had been cut in half by sickness. With the Union posing a renewed threat, the Florida regiments were sent to watch enemy movements west of Frankfort and to guard against any disruption of plans to install a Confederate government in Frankfort. Colonel Davis communicated situation reports by telegraph to General Kirby Smith in Lexington.

General Braxton Bragg, on the 28th, left his headquarters at Bardstown and went to Lexington to confer with Kirby Smith concerning their strategy and the planned installation of a new governor in Frankfort. On October 4th, Generals Bragg and Smith were in Frankfort to attend the inauguration of Richard Hawes as Confederate governor of Kentucky, but the ceremonies were cut short by reports of cannonading on the outskirts of the town. Union forces had started their offensive against the Rebels and were aiming to recapture Frankfort and Lexington, and then move against Bragg's army at Bardstown. General Bragg was feeling the heat of the Federals, so he ordered his entire corps at Bardstown to move eastward and link up with Kirby Smith's command. Major Footman turned his cavalry south and was kept busy watching the Yankee advance. Footman's men began ripping up rails and cutting telegraph wires in an effort to deny communications to the enemy. At the same instant, the dismounted companies, along with the other Florida regiments, had packed up and shifted to a line west of Lexington near Versailles. Footman's 1st Florida Squadron was moving well in the front of this line with eyes on the enemy.

The 1st Florida Cavalry Regiment commenced a forced march on October 6th from Versailles and concentrated with the main brigade at Herrodsburg. Footman's squadron soon joined the main body to await further instructions. Footman reported that he still had *"many men sick"* but that his squadron*" had suffered few deaths."*

When the Confederates evacuated Frankfort and Lexington, they left behind hundreds of sick soldiers. Cornelius C. Williamson, of the Florida Cavalry, volunteered to stay behind in a Lexington hospital to care for the sick soldiers who could not be evacuated. Corporal James Futch remained behind at Versailles to care for his sick brother, William, and another soldier, John Pollock, both privates of K Company.

By October 7th, the Yankees had reached Doctors Creek, south of Herrodsburg near Perryville. The season was extremely arid and the Union troops were dry from their long march. The water of Doctors Creek presented a thirst quenching invitation, except that it was ruled by Rebel sharpshooters. Throughout the night the Northern soldiers made assaults for the watering hole, only to be repulsed each time by a round of Confederate fire. The fight over creek water was the prelude to the Battle of Perryville. On the morning of October 8th, the Federals launched a full assault against the Rebels. The First Florida Cavalry was not in the main battle at Perryville, but was later subjected to light skirmishing as the Confederate army began withdrawing from the field toward Bryantsville. Both sides left the field at Perryville without a decisive victory.

On October 13th, the Confederates began their withdrawal from Kentucky taking with them an enormous bounty of captured goods in what was described as one of the oddest military convoys of the Civil War. The wagon train consisted of confiscated stage coaches, private carriages, a couple of hearses, buck boards, and over 400 brand new Union army wagons filled to the brim with captured supplies. Many of the soldiers were detailed as "*cowboys*" to keep droves of captured sheep, hogs, mules, and cattle, moving with the strange caravan.

The Rebels were going out of Kentucky by the same route they had come in, over Big Hill and through the mountains. None of this business had gone unnoticed by the Yankees, who were maintaining a close pursuit. The Florida Cavalrymen were among those sent to stretch a line of security along the mountainous path. The steady stream of wagons and troops, was constantly harassed by skirmishers throughout the rugged journey.

William Footman's mounted squadron had remained behind, north of Frankfort, performing guerrilla operations against the Union's rear. These First Cavalry troopers maneuvered dangerously behind the lines without logistical support and over a hundred miles from the main body of the Confederate army. Between October 15th and 20th, the First Florida Squadron operated in and around Gallatin, Henry, and Owen counties, cutting telegraph wires, burning bridges, and generally disrupting vital support lines to the Federal army. But their success in disabling enemy communications had not been ignored and on the night of October 16th, a detachment of the 57th Michigan Infantry surprised Footman's men with an ambush near Monterey, Kentucky. In this affair, five First Florida Cavalrymen were captured, along with their horses and accouterments. Research indicates that these Floridians were Bennett Osteen, John Mathers, Lewis Hogan, Will Newman, and 19 year old Rupert Charles. Colonel Orlando Moore, commander of the 57th Michigan, reported that "*three were let go due to ill health.*" Rupert Charles, according to the records, "*was never heard from again,*" and probably died as an unknown Florida Confederate soldier somewhere behind enemy lines. Footman's First Florida Mounted Squadron undoubtedly performed one of the most heroic and dangerous missions of the Kentucky campaign.

Satisfied that the main Confederate corps was well on its way out of Kentucky, the Yankees gave up their chase when the Rebels crossed over the Rock Castle River. The dismounted men of the First Florida Cavalry, reached Flat Rock, Kentucky, on the 20th, and by the next night were bivouaced at Cumberland Ford. It appears, from a soldier's letter, that some of the men took time to cook a decent meal, *"We staid the night by the ford on the cumberland and some boys from Hughes company got some salt pork and yanke meal from one of the wagons and fixed a fine supper and I went over and ate with sergt. Gold."* Although not proven, there are two reasons to believe that this information by an unknown writer, refers to Company K.; the name *Hughes*, could refer to either Captain David Hughes, or Lieutenant William Hughes, and Sergeant Gold was probably 4th Sergeant Andrew J. Gold, all members of Company K.

Major Stockton did not remain at Cumberland Ford, he was continued on to Cumberland Gap, 15 miles away, to prepare a camp for stragglers.

The First Florida Cavalry had paid a heavy price during the invasion of Kentucky. At least eight of the Regiment's men had died on the march to Lexington, sixty had been left behind sick, nearly all of whom ended up in enemy hands. Many of those taken prisoners later died in Northern prison camps. The number of actual battle casualties of the Regiment, based on available records, was less than a dozen wounded or killed.

The Confederate army moved into Cumberland Gap, which had been vacated by the Yankees at the beginning of the Kentucky campaign. The First Florida Cavalry dismounted soldiers began setting up camp and were soon assigned to routine camp and guard duties. They had hardly settled in before the Brigade was ordered to Blaines Crossroads, about 18 miles north of Knoxville. It is not clear what mission they performed at Blaines Crossroads, but after only a brief stay, they were marched back, *"through a heavy falling snow,"* to their winter camp at Cumberland Gap.

Meanwhile, Footman's mounted squadron was still back in Kentucky, trying to weave their way back to Tennessee without running into any Union patrols. With winter fast approaching, the trees had shed their foliage, leaving little concealment for the men as they rode through snow flurries toward the safety of the Tennessee border.

On the first of November, Major William Footman and his mounted squadron made it to the Gap and rejoined the rest of the Regiment.

FIRST FLORIDA CAVALRY REGIMENT CASUALTIES
OF THE KENTUCKY CAMPAIGN

++++✕✕✕✕✕✕✕✕++++

William Anderson, *died of disease*
Louis Appel, *captured,*
Thomas Ashley, *died of sickness*
William Barber, *left sick and captured*
William Barker, *captured*
Hiram Beasley, *left sick*
Kinchen Bell, *captured*
John Braddock, *died of disease*
James A. Brock, *left sick*
Ezekiel Bryant, *left sick and captured*
E. C. Chalker, *left sick and captured*
Rupert Charles, *left sick and missing*
Lanier C. Crafton, *left sick and captured*
George R. David, *left sick and captured*
John Davis, *left lame and captured*
Lawson Davis, *wounded and captured*
Lewis Davis, *wounded and captured*
Thomas Davis, *killed in action*
William Dickerson, *left sick status unknown*
William Dowling, *captured*
Benjamin Drew, *captured*
Matthew Ennis, *captured*
Patrick H. Forson, *captured*
James Futch, *left sick and captured*
William Futch, *left sick and captured*
Murdock Gillis, *left sick and captured*
M.G. Gillas, *captured*
Claiborn Ginan, *captured*
James T. Given, *captured*
William Cooper Goff, *left sick and captured*
Thomas Sam Goodbread, *left sick and captured*
Joseph Haddock, *died of disease*
James Harrell, *left sick*
David Harvil, *captured*
Henry H. Herring, left *sick and captured*
William A.J. Howard, *killed in action*
Henry Hunter, *captured*
Lewis Hogan, *captured*
Thomas Holton, *left behind and captured*
John Jarvis, *wounded*
John Johns, *captured*
Reuben Johns, *captured*

29.

Moses Johnson, *left sick and captured*
Robert W. Kelly, *left sick and captured*
Irving Kinard, *injured arm*
Baxter Leach, *missing*
Jesse Lee, *left lame and captured*
Jesse Lofton, *left sick*
Albert Martin, *captured*
John Mathers, *captured*
Frederick Lucius Merritt, *captured*
William M. Newman, *captured*
Clinton Neal, *left sick and missing*
Sanders Nobles, *left sick-died*
Bennett Osteen, *left sick and captured*
John Peacock, *left sick and captured*
Jefferson J. Philpot, *accidentally killed*
James Pickett, *captured*
John Pollock *captured*
Temple Powell, *left sick and captured*
Thomas Redding, *died of disease*
David Roberts, *left sick and captured*
Wiley Robson, *left sick and captured*
William Scarbourough, *captured*
Wilson Scott, *wounded and captured*
Henry F. Simmons, *left behind and captured*
Simeon A. Smith, *left sick and captured*
Simon P. Smith, *captured*
William L. Smith, *left sick, status unknown*
James Spencer, *died of disease*
Joshua Tanner, *died of disease*
Thomas R. Tedder, *left behind*
Daniel Thomas, *captured*
William Absolam Townsend, *captured*
Andrew Varnes, *captured*
Isham Walker, *left sick*
Robert W. Walker, *captured*
Richard Waters, *left behind and captured*
Cornelius C. Williamson, *captured*
George Wright, *left sick and captured*
Jesse Yelvington, *left sick and captured*

NOTE: Poor sanitation, contaminated drinking water, improper nutrition, fatigue, exposure, close living conditions, and scarcity of medical resources, all contributed to the high rates of sickness during the campaign. Records, for the most part, do not specify the kinds of diseases that plagued the individual Florida soldier. However, according to most records, the common afflictions during the Kentucky campaign were measles, dysentery, chronic diarrhea, lice, chiggers, mumps, rheumatism, bacterial infections, typhoid, bronchitis, intestinal disorders, small pox, pneumonia, colds, scurvy, varied foot ailments, and "continued fevers."

CHAPTER FOUR

FROM THE GAP TO THE RIDGE

 $\mathcal{A}$ blanket of snow covered Cumberland Gap as the Confederate army went about constructing winter quarters. Most of the First Florida Cavalry soldiers had never experienced snow, let alone the frozen harshness of a Cumberland winter.

On November 4th, 1862, Major Stockton was promoted to lieutenant-colonel and was assigned to administrative duties in Knoxville. Colonel William G. M. Davis, the founding father of the Regiment, was promoted to brigadier-general and placed in charge of the Department of East Tennessee. Lieutenant-Colonel Maxwell was promoted to full colonel and continued serving as commander of the First Florida Cavalry Regiment.

On November 7th, Major William Footman requested forage from the quartermaster for 137 horses. There are no records that indicate the number of men remaining in Footman's mounted squadron, but a later requisition shows Footman drawing rations for 110 men. On December 21st, he drew $576.30 in commutation of rations for 113 men at the rate of 30 cents per day for each man, for seventeen days. Other records indicate an aggregate strength of 211 men in the three mounted companies making up the squadron. That figure is probably inflated by failing to discount transfers, desertions, infirmed cases, discharges, and etc. The total regiment strength, mounted and dismounted, during this period was about 595, including ineffectives and unavailable troops. Actual effective fighting strength was probably half of the reported strength figures.

The three mounted companies performed short range patrols from their base at Cumberland Gap and frequently brought in a few captured bushwhackers. They continued their patrols until early December when they were assigned as a mounted guard at Sugar Rum and Fulkerson Gaps. During this period the snow was so deep that the mounted companies were cut off from the main Regiment at Cumberland Gap. The dismounted companies at the Gap were trying to endure the freezing cold without adequate clothing and shoes. They had no tents and there were no axes, or other tools, for constructing decent shelters. Some had salvaged a few scraps of lumber which had been left by the Yankees when they evacuated the Gap. The snow had covered any chance of finding fire wood, leaving the soldiers with a cruel choice of building shelters or burning lumber to keep warm. Several of the men were sick with fevers and pneumonia, and a few had already died. The staff officers faired much better, most were headquartered in Knoxville boarding houses, well away from the misery at Cumberland Gap. Colonel Jesse J. Finley, of the 6th Florida Infantry, on duty in Knoxville, expressed compassion for all the Floridians at Gap and formally requested to *"move the Florida boys south."* But Colonel Finley's hopes for his fellow Floridians were never realized; the men would just have to suffer the bone chilling winter.

Some relief came in mid-December when the Floridians were ordered to Kingston, where they made camp in the fork of the Tennessee and

Clinch rivers. After their duty at Kingston, the Regiment was moved to Morristown, then to Knoxville, and finally northeast to Strawberry Plains. However, the three mounted companies were still at Cumberland Gap, where they continued to conduct raids along the Kentucky border and into North Carolina. According to a January 3, 1864 supply requisition, Major Footman requested 2000 rounds of Enfield ammunition. In late January, the mounted squadron received 47 new saddles, 57 new bridles, and 53 horse blankets from the quartermaster depot at Knoxville.

When it was reported that the enemy might make a move on the Gap, the mounted Floridians were ordered to join the main Regiment garrisoned at Strawberry Plains. Here, on February 18th, twenty men of Company A, of the Squadron, were dismounted, along with ten each from E and F companies. Some of these soldiers were discharged and others were reassigned to the dismounted companies at Strawberry Plains, which were attached to Brigadier General Alfred E. Jackson's brigade under the Department of East Tennessee.

In the middle of March, the mounted squadron was sent on a mission across the Kentucky border to disrupt the enemy's lines of communication. The Squadron's horses were in poor condition and the ride was hard. Asa B. Smith's mount came up lame and had to be abandoned. James M. Giles and William F. Gwaltney, both of Company F, and George Lewis of Company E, also lost their horses during the ride. Then the Squadron ran into an unexpected enemy force near Somerset, Kentucky. Richard Slauter was among the first to fall to Yankee fire, David Whigham and George Tully had their horses shot down. Berry Goodman was shot in the hip and Sergeant William S. Bugg was hit in the shoulder. Bugg struggled for cover but was eventually captured along with Private Wiley L. Koon. This single affair claimed the lives of John Herrod, Abram Youngblood, William Jackson, and Virgil Renfroe. Lieutenant Martin I. Cox was captured while commanding Company A. [Cox was sent to Fort Delaware but was only confined until April 25th, when he was released on parole]. Stephen D. Bell, of Company F, was wounded and captured by the enemy. [Bell was shipped off to the Fort Henry prison]. Two rounds penetrated the chest and leg of Wilson Scott as his horse was shot from under him. The Yankees wasted no time in capturing Scott, but John Burnett and 3rd Sergeant Joshua Lee, both seriously injured, managed to escape. Corporal Thomas Walston was listed as missing in the action and was never heard from again. The costly contest had weakened the Squadron's fighting ability as a mounted force.

The surviving troopers limped back to Wartburg, Tennessee, to lick their wounds and reorganize. Major Footman looked at his once gallant cavalry squadron, there were few men left, and hardly any fit horses. Between May 1st and 15th, the remaining horsemen of the Squadron were dismounted. These men reorganized as dismounted companies and rejoined the main regiment to serve as infantry. Although William Footman had served gallantly and with great service, he was not reelected during this reorganization. In early June, Footman volunteered as a staff aide to Brigadier General Pegram's cavalry. He then applied for a regular appointment to major of cavalry and requested reassignment to the First Florida Cavalry Regiment. William Footman's request was only partially filled, on December 23, 1864, he was officially promoted to the rank of major but was reassigned to the Florida Special Cavalry Battalion, with the mission of protecting Florida's cattle herds against Union raiders. On February 20, 1865, Major William Footman led 275 soldiers of the Cow Cavalry in a daring assault against Union infantry at Fort Myers.

Between March and June 1863, various detachments of the First Florida Cavalry Regiment were involved in action at Wartburg, Lenoir, Powell's Valley, Roger's Gap, and Montgomery, Tennessee. U. S.General Burnsides had sent brigades of cavalry and infantry with the objective of capturing Knoxville. The dismounted Florida cavalrymen would spend their summer constantly employed in a series of defensive actions as part of the Tullahoma campaign.

Lt. Colonel William Stockton speculated in a letter home, that due to conditions, *"that Colonel Scott, if appointed brigadier general, would be bound to remount the regiment and have it join his brigade."* The hopes of remounting the Florida men seems to have never faded, unfortunately they were destined to walk their way through the rest of the war.

In early June 1863, the First Florida Cavalry, now stationed at Loudon as part of General Bate's brigade, was shifted to Hoover's Gap to counter a reported enemy advance at Stones River. On June 26th, the Regiment was involved in affairs against elements of General George H. Thomas' Union forces. They were employed in heavy skirmishing until ordered to pull back with General Alexander Stewart's division. The Floridians were immediately moved to Tullohoma as the Union army continued its advance in two columns; one aimed at Knoxville and the other at Chattanooga.

Lt. Colonel Stockton was in Knoxville, living in his office beneath the Lamar House, with his Black servant, Ned, and eating at the Franklin hotel. He wrote in a letter to his wife, *"There is so much that I dislike in our regiment that I do not care to serve in it except as a matter of duty."* Stockton was taking care of administrative duties for the Regiment and was assisted by 2nd Lt. Henry Horne. As with all supplies, paper, pens, and ink, were scarce. Sugar was a $1.00 a pound, butter $1.50, and cornmeal sold for $3.50. The cost of lodging in Knoxville was so inflated that Stockton complained in a letter about his rent, *"board is $150 a month, I'll camp in the woods first."*

On August 24th, William Stockton rejoined the Regiment at Loudon, southwest of Knoxville. A few days later, the Federals began putting pressure on Loudon, forcing the Rebels to pull back. They began moving south and after a hard three day march reached a point forty miles above Chattanooga. The Regiment set up camp between Charleston and Georgetown. Contrary to his previous complaints about the Regiment, Colonel Stockton wrote, *"Our little Regiment is in the finest possible order and marched like soldiers, I think they will fight back--they have every confidence in their officers."*

On September 6th, Union forces moved into Knoxville and captured a large number of Southern troops. Three days later, and 114 miles to the south, Union troops grabbed control of Chattanooga and forced the Confederates to retreat into Georgia. The 55,000 strong enemy force, led by Rosecrans, was intent on pushing the Rebels farther south, but the

Confederates were soon reinforced with 70,000 troops from Virginia. General Braxton Bragg then turned his attention to subduing the Yankee threat. The First Florida Cavalry, still under Colonel George T. Maxwell, was moved to near Missionary Ridge and reassigned to Trigg's Brigade of Preston's Division, in Buckner's Corps. Braxton Bragg, now with superior strength, began planning his strategy to eradicate the Federals. The First Cavalry was ordered to clean their weapons and stand ready to march.

At daybreak, on September 19th, the First Florida Cavalrymen moved with Trigg's Brigade across Chickamauga Creek and took up a line near the Hunt house. This line was an extension of General Bate's battle line. As the Floridians prepared for battle, Union artillery opened up from a battery on their right. Upon encountering heavy shot and shell, the brigade quickly advanced forward seeking cover beneath a hill. Colonel Maxwell was then ordered to move his First Florida Cavalry 300 yards forward of the main line as skirmishers. The Florida troops were greeted with heavy fire from enemy infantry and artillery. The fight went on for nearly two hours in a corn field and in the nearby woods, until grape and canister shot forced them to withdraw. The Florida cavalrymen then rejoined the main brigade as it was shifted to support Brigadier General Robertson's troops under Hood's command. As Trigg's Brigade moved along a fence line, they were hit with cannon and rifle fire from well entrenched enemy positions. The brigade continued their advance, laying down a strong field of fire that caused the Yankees to pull back in confusion. Lt. Richard Hart, of E Company was killed in the fighting. The First Florida Cavalry suffered two killed, fifteen wounded, and one reported missing in action.

The next morning, September 20th, the brigade was sent to backup Manigault's brigade. After encountering no enemy response to artillery fire, the brigade was ordered to provide support to William's Confederate artillery batteries. After about two hours, the First Florida Cavalry and the 7th Florida Infantry, were ordered to pull back and provide a rear guard against an anticipated Union cavalry attack. The Floridians took up positions near LaFayette Road, expecting the Federals to approach from the direction of Lee and Gordon's Mill. When the Union cavalry failed to show, the Floridians were ordered to return to their brigade, now engaged with the enemy on a ridge. However, in the process of making their way back, the First Florida Cavalry was diverted to support General Gracie's Brigade involved at Snodgrass Hill. As the Florida soldiers moved at quick time through the smoke filled woods, they were continuously challenged by enemy rifles on a ridge line. They crossed several open fields scattered with dead clad in both blue and gray. As they pressed forward through a ravine, the men ignored the dead and the hateful smell of burnt powder, but could not shut out the moans of the recent wounded. *"I saw shot men holding there* [sic] *insides in there hands,"* recalled a veteran of the horror, *"one had his eye hanging out & another poor boy was cut in 2 peeces* [sic], *he was still alive & begging & laid there waving his arm at us in the air."*

Upon reaching General Gracie in the late afternoon, the exhausted First Cavalry troops were ordered to assault enemy breastworks on a hill. Gracie's men, a much larger force, had already been thrown back twice. Colonel Maxwell protested that his smaller force of Floridians could hardly be expected to do much better. Maxwell was ordered to hold his troops in the area until Gracie could reorganize his brigade. The First Cavalry men waited in position, but were soon exposed to heavy fire and had to fall back to the security of a rail fence. They later joined with Gracie's troops in the famous assault against Snodgrass Hill. In this last day of fighting, the 1st Cavalry lost one man killed and nine wounded, with Lieutenant-Colonel Stockton and Captain Gaston Finley being among the wounded.

Regimental Casualties and Men Cited for Gallantry at Chickamauga.

Arrick, Thomas H. wounded

Beach, John M., wounded

Beck, R.D. wounded

Corbin, James W. wounded

Dobson, Benjamin, wounded

Ellison, Joshua H., wounded

Finley, Gaston, Capt. wounded

Goddard, Harvey J. wounded in arm
HONOR ROLL for Gallantry

Grimes, John,
HONOR ROLL for Gallantry

Hagin, Peter T. J. wounded

Hart, Richard, Lt. killed

Harvey, John W., wounded

Herring, John W. killed,
HONOR ROLL for Gallantry

Higginbothem, Madison,
HONOR ROLL for Gallantry

Johns, James W. wounded

Johnson, Luke, wounded

Johnson, William, wounded

Johnson, Stephen S., died of wounds

Lewis, George, wounded
HONOR ROLL for Gallantry

Maxwell, David Elwell, wounded

Philips, Riley, wounded lost arm
HONOR ROLL for Gallantry

Rollins, John D., wounded

Simmons, Moses, wounded
HONOR ROLL for Gallantry

Smith, Edward, wounded

Stanton, George W. wounded

Stockton, William, Lt.Col. wounded

Swift, Joseph, wounded

Thomas, Daniel D. wounded

Tully, George W.,
HONOR ROLL for Gallantry

Tyner, Edward,
HONOR ROLL for Gallantry

Wainwright, Edward J. wounded

Walker, James I., wounded

Waters, Richard, wounded

Weeks, James T., wounded

Chickamauga, one of the greatest battles of the war, had ended in a Confederate victory. However, General Braxton Bragg failed to follow up on his success and allowed the badly mauled Union army to escape into Chattanooga; a shortcoming that would eventually deny the Southern troops the fruits of their well earned victory.

General Rosecrans wasted no time in reorganizing his Union army in Chattanooga and made preparations to hold out until his forces could be replenished. The Yankees immediately stretched a defensive line between the city and the Confederates. The Rebels established a siege line extending along Missionary Ridge and across to Lookout Mountain. By October, the Union army was experiencing severe logistical problems in Chattanooga. They were running short on medical supplies, food, fuel, ammunition, clothing, and were having to live on hard bread. From Chattanooga, Union officers watched the signals between Bragg's headquarters on Missionary Ridge and the Rebel positions on Lookout Mountain. In Washington, authorities had already ordered a sizable reinforcement for Rosecrans. A Union force of 20,000 troops and 3000 horses was already on the rails to Chattanooga. By November 15th, 17,000 Federal reinforcements had arrived at Bridgeport, Alabama. Braxton Bragg, expecting the Yankees to vacate Chattanooga, delayed taking any offensive action. In early October, after figuring out that the enemy intended to remain in place, General Bragg finally ordered raids against the Yankee supply lines to the city.

On the 23rd, General U. S. Grant arrived to manage the situation in Chattanooga and replaced General Rosecrans with General Thomas as commander of the Union Army of the Cumberland. The Confederates had successfully blocked the enemy's supply channel to Chattanooga. But the Yankees, thanks to their chief engineer, General William "Baldy" Smith, promptly figured out a way to bypass the Rebel blockade with a new supply route. This new link to Federal supply resources, was called the "Cracker Line." It did not take long before rations and ammunition were again flowing into Chattanooga.

While the Union army was fattening itself on reinforcements and supplies, its leaders were drawing up plans for a major offensive against the Confederates. On the 15th of November, General William T. Sherman arrived in Chattanooga for a strategy briefing with General Grant.

Meanwhile, the First Florida Cavalry was camped near Chickamauga creek. The weather had been rainy and the roads so bad that hundreds of Rebel wagons were having a hard time pulling through the mud. Some wagons were short on mule teams and a few teamsters had remedied their situation by stealing mules from teams belonging to other regiments. William A. Cox, a teamster with the First Florida Cavalry, reported that one of his wagon mules had been stolen. The mule, one of four hitched to a supply wagon, was never found and may have ended up hitched to a wagon of another regiment. With the roads in such poor shape, a company of pioneers was assigned to cut and lay a new road to the main commissary at Chickamauga Station. To the joy of the troops, a good quantity of beef began arriving almost daily from Florida. In addition to meat, many of the Florida men were issued new English blankets, which according to Washington Ives, *"Were as big as a double bed."*

On November 12th, by Special Order Number 294, all the remnants of the Florida regiments, previously under Trigg's and Stovall's brigades, were consolidated into a single brigade in General Bate's Division. The new brigade was designated as the *"Florida Brigade"* and was placed under the command of newly promoted Brigadier-General Jesse J. Finley. The Florida Brigade, also known as *"Finley's Brigade,"* was made up from the following regiments; the 1st and 3rd Florida Infantries, commanded by Col. William S. Dillsworth, The 4th Florida Infantry, commanded by Colonel W. L. Bowen, The 6th Florida Infantry, commanded by Lt. Col. Angus D. McLean, The 7th Florida Infantry, commanded by Col. Robert Bullock, and The 1st Florida Cavalry Regiment dismounted, commanded by Col. George T. Maxwell.

[NOTE: *There were two "Florida Brigades" during the Civil War, the subject one and another which was formed from the 2nd, 5th, and 8th Florida Infantry Regiments in the Army of Northern Virginia. The latter brigade was later combined with remnants of the 9th, 10th, and 11th, Florida Infantries to form what became known as "Finegan's Brigade"*].

The Florida regiments had been so devastated by losses that most were not much larger than company size. The First Florida Cavalry Regiment, which had initially organized with nearly a thousand mounted men, had been reduced to a mere 200 dismounted soldiers.

On November 24th, the Florida Brigade was placed into positions to the right of Bragg's headquarters on top of Missionary Ridge. Three of its regiments, the 1st Florida Cavalry, the 4th and 7th Florida Infantries, were sent down to the bottom of the ridge to prepare and hold a picket line in the Chattanooga Valley. The trenches along this line were in voice range of the enemy. The landscape separating the two opposing forces, was strewn with brush and fallen timbers. Behind the Floridia men, the steep wall of Missionary Ridge rose upward 700 feet above the valley. About halfway up was a second line of intrenchments, and above this was the crest of the ridge, fortified with batteries containing fifty-six guns. The First Cavalry and 4th Florida regiments were so positioned as to be the first in line for an enemy assault, but their orders *"were to hold at all hazards."* In retrospect it was a suicidal trap with no means of reinforcing or withdrawing the troops in the event of an attack.

At 3:40, on the afternoon of November 25th, Union guns fired a signal and twenty thousand Yankee infantrymen began pouring toward the base of Missionary Ridge. The plan was to take only the Rebel picket line at the base of the Ridge, however, the order was miscommunicated in General Sheridan's division to mean *"Take everything in front of you."* This caused a massive assault that would not stop until it reached the very top of Missionary Ridge. The Floridians at the base were the first to feel the heat; they braced themselves for the attack but were soon forced to flee their trenches. They fought hand to hand in a struggle up the steep, rugged slopes while praying to survive long enough to reach the next line of defenses. At the top of the ridge the order went out for Finley to pull back his First Cavalry and 4th Infantry troops, but General Breckenridge intervened and directed that the Floridians remain in place. In a desperate attempt to save their own lives, the Floridians threw away their equipment and began scrambling up the mountain side. The air was thick with musket balls as both Rebels and Yankees went over the second line of trenches together. Lt. Colonel Stockton, weak from illness, fell exhausted and could not make the climb. Two Florida boys stopped to help him, but both were shot dead in a hail of bullets. Lieutenant Stevens fell dead half way up the hill and James Cook, of Company F, was mortally wounded. Three soldiers grabbed Cook and began dragging his lifeless body to the top. The guns on the crest were useless, they could only over shoot the affair beneath them. The artillerymen began rolling cannon balls and rocks down the side at the enemy, but only succeeded in hitting some of the escaping Floridians. Private William Hawkins, of Company K, to lighten his load, tossed away his Enfield rifle and accouterments. He then found cover behind a boulder where he hugged the ground until the enemy had passed on up the slope.

It took nearly an hour of chaotic terror for the Floridians to reach the crest, where they soon realized that most of their comrades, and all of their field officers, had fallen into enemy hands. Upon reaching the top, the Rebels were scattered in confusion, and without their leadership there was no way to organize a defensive action against the overpowering Federals. By nightfall the Union army was in control of Missionary Ridge and the Confederates were hastily withdrawing off the ridge. As General Bragg and his staff, rode off toward Chickamauga Station, General Finley was ordered to take the 6th Florida and set up a rear guard to delay the enemy's pursuit. Finley's Floridians managed to turn the enemy, which bought needed time for the Southern army to vacate the mountain.

It was well after dark before the firing ceased, many Confederates were still wandering around in the darkness trying to locate their regiments. The few surviving First Florida Cavalry troops were so scattered that some remained missing for days. The Florida Brigade teamsters headed the wagons toward Resaca as the troops marched at quick time on Ringgold road in the direction of Tunnel Hill. The Brigade, minus over half of its men, arrived the next day near Dalton, Georgia.

General Bate, in his official report, states that his command lost 43 killed, 224 wounded, and 590 missing, of which at least 167 of the missing and casualties were from the 1st Florida Cavalry. The Union had captured all of the First Cavalry's staff and field officers. First Cavalry colonels

Maxwell and Stockton, with the 7th Florida commander, Colonel Bullock, and Captains Finley, Shine and B. M. Burroughs, along with Lieutenant Footman, were all among the prisoners. The captives were herded immediately to the Chattanooga railroad yards, where most were sent on to the Johnson Island prison camp, near Sandusky, Ohio.

Almost all of the surviving soldiers of the First Cavalry later faced disciplinary action for abandoning their arms and accouterments during their escape from certain death at the base of Missionary Ridge. General Bate had recommended punishment, and payment for the value of the equipment lost by each man. However, it appears that no one was ever actually penalized. A Board of Inquiry reviewed each case and found that the losses of personal equipment and rifles, were unavoidable under the circumstances.

December was turning into another bone chilling winter for the Floridians. The brigade began building their winter quarters near Dalton. The 1st Cavalry and 4th Florida Regiments, began constructing crude log huts near the railroad line, about a mile from town. The men scavenged for old pine logs or whatever could be found for building material. The huts, sealed with daubs of mud and varying in size and looks, accommodated from two to six men. Discarded barrels and boxes added the luxury of furniture. *"To spite of the rain,"* penned one soldier, *"...our hut is purty warm and we had some biled rice & roasted acurns for supper."*

In a letter to Lt. Colonel Stockton's wife, dated December 7, 1863, Joseph S. M. Davidson wrote from Dalton, *"Last evening two commissioned officers of this command, Knight & Roberts, who were captured at the late battle of Missionary Ridge, arrived in this camp having escaped the enemy. They convey the information that Col. Stockton, Bullock, & Maxwell & Captains Shine, Burroughs, and indeed all our officers captured were unhurt with the exception of Lt. Stevens of the 1st Florida (dismounted) who was mortally wounded."* Davidson then added, *"...the officers returned report that our officers were getting along very well indeed being as well treated by the enemy as could possibly be expected from such vile scamps."*

The winter at Dalton was peaceful, the cold and rain had denied either side any military opportunities. Yet Sherman's army, like a frozen menace waiting to thaw, was only a short distance to the north. In the meantime, the Florida soldiers, when not on picket duty, huddled around their fires playing cards and telling stories of past battles in this long war. On occasion a local preacher would drop by *"...to spread the good word,"* said one private, *"...which some needed due to their excessiveness of gambling & drinking."* The Rebels concocted a fermented brew from pine boughs which they called *"pine top,"* most likely the featured drink on that lonely Christmas night of 1863. *"Some were too much tipsy, but I went in forenoon to church in Dalton with a boy from the Florida camp,"* wrote a Kentucky soldier who described Christmas Day as *"...cloudy and raining."*

There were four churches in Dalton that were *"As generally full to overflowing on Sundays with soldiers,"* wrote one soldier to his father, *"Many soldiers go to church just to get sight of a lady."*

On December 27th, General Joseph E. Johnston arrived at Dalton to replace Braxton Bragg as commander of the Army of Tennessee. Johnston found his new command to be severely deficient in men, arms, supplies, and with horses too feeble for use. General Joe Johnston, after looking over his new command, remarked, "...*the number of bare feet was painful to see.*" The General immediately implemented plans to bring the Army of Tennessee up to acceptable standards. He restored discipline, clothed the ragged soldiers and put shoes on bare feet. Over half of the First Florida Cavalry men had been without adequate foot wear, many had no shoes at all, and few had warm clothing. General Johnston's efforts to resupply his troops was a welcomed relief for the men of the Florida Brigade.

On January 21, 1864, the Florida Brigade was formed with the Army of Tennessee on the field for an inspection by General Johnston and General Hardee. The improvements in morale and discipline were remarkable; the great Army of Tennessee was looking like a fighting force again. On January 30th, General Hardee conducted a readiness inspection of Bate's Division and observed the Florida Brigade conducting maneuvers.

On February 5th, Johnston ordered a grand review of the entire army on a large field south of Dalton. The regiments were formed in three parallel lines which stretched nearly two miles. General Joe Johnston rode his horse up and down the ranks, paying close attention to the condition of the men. When he finished his inspection, the General took a position front and center of his army and watched as the troops paraded in review. The First Florida Cavalry soldiers proudly led the Florida Brigade in the parade.

The 1st Florida Cavalry and 4th Florida Infantry regiments, were so severely reduced in numbers that the two regiments were officially united into a single regiment. Lt. Colonel Edward Badger, commander of the 4th Florida Infantry Regiment, was put in charge of the newly consolidated 1st Cavalry and 4th Infantry regiment. The war had taken such a terrible toll on the Floridians that after consolidation, these two regiments hardly equaled the strength of two regular size companies.

Confederate infantrymen on the battle line in the woods at Chickamauga.
From an 1888 illustration in *"Battles and Leaders of the Civil War.*

CHAPTER FIVE

THE ATLANTA CAMPAIGN

The first real action of 1864 for the Florida Brigade came in late February when it was ordered to proceed two miles west, near Creek Gap, as skirmishers to check a Federal advance. The 1st Florida Cavalry and 4th Infantry soldiers were placed forward in rifle pits and endured several days of heavy skirmishing in the cold and rain. They were relieved of this duty on the 28th and returned to the comfort of their huts at Dalton.

The inclement weather had turned their campground into a mire of red mud. A large number of soldiers were down with fevers and colds, but a new issue of rations and blankets brought a little relief in warmth and nourishment. While conditions had improved considerably under General Joe Johnston, the soldiers still looked like a tattered bunch and were physically worn by many battles. Mentally, they were hardened to just about any miserable situation and had endured more than their share.

In early March, a headquarters circular was passed to the brigade commanders ordering the regiments to be formed to witness an execution of one of their own. The Florida Brigade formed on the field with their division on the morning of March 2nd as reluctant observers to this affair. The unfortunate man, Private William Cork, was blindfolded and placed before the firing squad. Although the condemned man was not from the Florida Brigade, he served as a reminder of what could happen to any soldier who chose to violate army regulations. In this case, a simple charge of desertion had resulted in a death sentence. General Joe Johnston's message was clear, he expected total military obedience within the ranks of the Army of Tennessee. Private William Cork had become one more sad statistic in a this long war.

A week later, Lt. General William J. Hardee was appointed corps commander. Hardee's Corps consisted of Cheatham's Division, Walker's Division, Cleburne's Division, and Bate's Division, the latter under which was assigned Finley's Florida Brigade. Bate's Division had been recently substituted as a replacement for Stevenson's Division, which had been reassigned to General John Bell Hood's 2nd Corps.

Near the end of March the weather had cleared, but a thick blanket of late snow still covered the Florida camp at Dalton. To break the boredom of camp life, some of the boys from the 4th Kentucky and Tyler's Brigade, challenged the Florida Brigade with a barrage of snow balls. The Floridians began piling out of their huts to join in a mock battle against the assaulting snow ballers. They soon joined ranks with their friendly assailants and marched off across the hill for an attack on the boys of Stovall's Brigade. Generals Stovall and Stewart joined in the play and led their troops in a great snow ball war that lasted well into the evening. Years later, one old Kentucky veteran described the great snow ball battle as *"The best fun we ever had in the war."* The casualties were light, only a few bruises and cold nipped fingers, but for a brief moment, the great snow ball battle had offered a break in the routine of soldier life at Dalton.

The remainder of March, and into April, was spent working on fortifications around Dalton and playing *"town ball,"* sort of like an early version of baseball. The Florida regiments took their turns at picket duty and pulling guard duty at the depot in Dalton. Maneuver training continued, mostly close order drill and shooting at targets. Special attention was given to how fast a soldier could shoot and reload his weapon. In actual battle, an experience soldier could fire an average of about 20 to 30 rounds, unfortunately that rate also applied to the enemy.

On April 22nd, all furloughs were suspended due to a force of 15,000 Federals gathering about ten miles from Ringgold. The Rebels began preparing for a major defensive. By May 1st, Sherman's army was on the move again and four days later they were at Ringgold. General Johnston immediately dispatched an advance guard to the front which resulted in several straight days of skirmishing. The Federals successfully took Tunnel Hill, but quickly retreated. Then overnight, a heavy Union force moved up on the Cleveland road and went into position around Tunnel Hill. On Saturday, May 7th, the Florida men took one last look at their winter quarters and were marched off in the middle of the night to check the enemy. The Floridians, moving through Mill Creek Gap, formed a horseshoe shaped battle line in front of the Gap and within sight of the enemy positions on a ridge between Tunnel Hill and Dalton. When heavy firing broke out on the 8th, the Florida Brigade was moved to the mountain on the left of the Gap as Union skirmishers were deployed to the front of Mill Creek. The weather had turned bad with a soaking down pour of rain that filled the trenches, but the Rebels managed to throw back the enemy with a heavy loss. The next day Union skirmishers were deployed in front of the Florida Brigade and attempted an assault, but were once again forced back with Rebel yells and a hail of fire.

When the Federals began flanking movements around the Confederate lines, the Rebels were compelled to evacuate Dalton. General Johnston felt that he could find a better position to make a stand and began moving his troops toward Calhoun, Georgia. The Florida Brigade began the move on May 13th and marched nine miles past Cleburne's Division. They halted for a short rest at some old breastworks and then proceeded four more miles to Resaca. At this point, three companies from the 1st and 4th regiments were sent forward to establish a picket line to check any enemy advance. The next day, the three picket companies were driven back to the main line by Union infantry. In this confrontation, Private Jesse Lofton fell wounded on the field and the Florida Brigade commander, General Finley, was injured when he was struck by a tree limb snapped off by an incoming cannon ball. Finley was hauled to the rear and Colonel Bullock took command of the Florida Brigade. Bullock, who had been captured at Missionary Ridge, had recently rejoined his unit after being released through a prisoner exchange. In this latest action the Florida Brigade suffered some thirty casualties in killed and wounded.

The next day, the Florida Brigade found themselves holding the center of the Confederate line. The 1st Cavalry and 4th Infantry were on Hardee's right wing facing head-on against the 35th Ohio Infantry. The two sides, separated only by Camp creek, began skirmishing in early morning. The Floridians held their own until driven back by a small, but aggressive force. Meanwhile, the 1st and 7th Florida Infantries were fighting a brisk battle from nearby breastworks and had suffered considerably in wounded. The 1st Cavalry, 4th and 3rd Florida infantries, were pulled from the fighting and placed in reserve.

On May 15th, Bate's Division broke the morning calm with action against the enemy that lasted all day. By sundown, they had inflicted substantial losses on the opposition. Then, under the cover of darkness, Hardee began moving his entire corps to the south; crossing the Oostanaula River on the rail and wagon bridge. The Florida Brigade, after setting fire to the bridge, was among the last to cross. The enemy was moving close behind in a determined chase. The Florida regiments pressed on, marching to a point eight miles to the south. Here they were detailed to stand as a rear guard to discourage any Yankee followers. They drew a line of defense across Sherman's path at Calhoun, but Union cavalry soon forced the Southerners to withdraw.

That night, the Floridians took up a march in the rain, passing by Walker's Division as it held back enemy infantry. A couple of Georgia regiments pushed the Yankees into a brief retreat which gained enough time for the Rebels to head in the direction of Adairsville. The Confederate wagons, and soldiers, were mired down in knee deep mud as they followed the railroad through the rainy darkness to Adairsville.

On the morning of May 17th, the Floridians, dog tired and caked with mud, reached the outskirts of Adairsville. They tried to rest but were constantly interrupted by enemy sharpshooters. The afternoon was spent in hit and miss skirmishing. They formed a defensive line and threw up a quick breastwork of fence rails. Some of the Floridians moved forward slightly but had to quickly pull back to the safety of their works. During this fracas, John Jackson and Private Kelly were pinned down and ended up in the hands of an enemy infantry squad. When night came, the Florida Brigade was ordered to move again. Lt. Colonel Badger left two companies behind as rear guards with orders to follow up the next day and to collect any stragglers along the way. The main body of the Brigade marched all night and went into bivouac the next day about two miles from Kingston. This was part of a strategy designed by General Johnston to bait Sherman into turning his army toward Adairsville. The rest of the Army of Tennessee, Polk's and Hood's corps, had headed for Cassville. But Sherman, wise to the situation, divided his Federal corps between Adairsville and Cassville. The main Confederate force at Cassville soon found themselves engaged in combat, as Hardee's Corps, with the Florida Brigade awaited developments at Kingston.

At mid-morning on May 19th, the Yankees hit the Floridian's rear guard. By early afternoon the enemy had dug in for a fight as the Floridians erected a defensive work of logs. At 4 p.m., Major Jacob Lash took two hundred men from the 1st Cavalry and 4th Florida Infantry to defend the rear of Bate's Division. The fighting ceased later that evening, but the Floridians would not enjoy the luxury of sleep, instead they were ordered, at three in the morning, to move out toward the Etowah river. The 1st and 3rd Florida Infantries, under Major Ball, led the Brigade, with the 1st Cavalry and 4th Infantry bringing up the rear. The roads were axle deep in orange mud, offering little mercy to the wagons and tired feet. They crossed the river in late afternoon and proceeded three miles south where they set up camp. The Floridians remained there until May 23rd, when they were ordered to march toward Dallas, Georgia. They started out just before noon, it was a very warm day, and along the eight mile march they had several minor encounters with the enemy. On May 24th, the Brigade, at two in the morning and after marching six miles, rested briefly at New Hope Church. A drenching rain storm blew in just as they took up the march again, lasting until they arrived later the next night at Dallas. Knowing that the Federals were close, the Confederates began preparing entrenchments. In the dark of night, and in a heavy rain that had turned the ground into a slippery mess, the Floridians began digging in with tin pans, cups, and even their bare hands. Their trenches quickly became water filled ditches as they struggled to keep the sides from caving in. It seemed like the weather had joined the Yankees in making their lives miserable.

The next day, the Brigade began building breastworks while in the distance they could hear the mockery of a Yankee band playing "Dixie." At sunrise, on May 27th, extreme fighting broke out along the front as the Florida Brigade was ordered closer to Dallas. Their objective was to block an attempted westward maneuver by Sherman's three corps. Lt. William Gorman, of the 4th Florida, was wounded while in command of a picket line. Corporal Robert Partin, also of the 4th Florida, led a squad in repulsing some Yankee intruders who had infiltrated the Rebel picket line.

General Hardee assigned Bate's Division to feel out the Federal strength around Dallas. Bate prepared a plan to encircle the Union right at Dallas and instructed Colonel Bullock to advance his Floridians forward against the enemy. The Florida Brigade was joined in this cause by two other brigades and was cautioned to withdraw if they met strong resistance. Thomas Smith's Brigade was on Bate's left, and on the right was General Lewis' famed Kentucky Orphan Brigade. The Kentuckians moved hard against the enemy, but Bullock's Floridians were thrown back by heavily entrenched Union infantry. In the process of pulling back under heavy fire, Colonel Angus McLean, of the 6th Florida, was killed while leading his regiment. The next day was filled with artillery duels and brisk shooting. The Rebels unloaded sixteen cannons on Union positions, which led to the Northern troops calling the place, *"The hell hole."* The night before, while catching a brief rest, Lt. R. G. Shaw had a premonition that he would die in battle the next day. Strangely enough, Shaw was killed the next morning while in charge of his company. That same afternoon, at 3 o'clock, Finley's Florida Brigade was ordered to charge the fortifications of the enemy. The Floridians, according to an enemy soldier, *"Charged with heads bowed down and hats pulled down over their eyes, as if to hide from view their inevitable death."* The Yankees poured a murderous fire on the advancing Florida regiments, cutting their charge to pieces just fifty yards from the trenches of the 53rd and 37th Ohio infantries. Private Bond was among the first Floridians to be struck down, Lt James Kilpatrick, of the 4th Florida, received a mortal wound, he crawled to a log where he removed his belt and shoes, and then quietly succumbed to his injury. Private McLaird of the 6th Florida fell dead on the field and Private Webb, Corporal John Farnell, and Lt. George Dekle were all left in the hands of the enemy. Colonel Bullock then advanced the Brigade up the Marietta road to take on another enemy emplacement. Daniel Thomas caught a bullet in his leg and managed to limp to cover. Captain Martin Cox, while directing his cavalrymen, was shot in the knee; his brother, William, met with a similar fate when a ball tore into his leg. Private William C. Hawkins, of Company K, scrambled for a nearby log and took up a firing position next to Henry Crews. Hawkins leveled his Enfield rifle on the log and was about to squeeze off a shot when a Yankee round ripped off his trigger finger and penetrated his wrist. The Federals had hit Bate's Division with a devastating blow leaving 450 Rebel casualties on the battlefield. At least six of the killed and wounded were from the First Florida Cavalry. Following the battle, Lt. Daniel Knight, with a squad of men, was ordered to retrieve the wounded. In the process Knight was captured, along with his squad consisting of Privates Coleman, Stokeley, Brooks, and Nettles. They were escorted to the nearest railroad and put on a train for Nashville. But, near Stevenson, Alabama, Lt. Knight managed to jump off the train and later made his way back to the 1st Cavalry Regiment. The other men were sent on to the Rock Island prison camp, where they remained for the duration of the war.

Private John K. Duke, of the 53rd Ohio Regiment, later noted, "*The charge of the Florida Brigade* [at Dallas] *was an extremely gallant one.*" Duke's observation, considering that it comes from a veteran of the other side, is a testimonial to the Florida Brigade's bravery.

Most of the Florida casualties from the Battle of Dallas were sent to Bragg Hospital at Newnan, Georgia, where Ward Number 5 was referred to as "*The Florida Hospital.*" Doctor Steele, formerly with the 3rd Florida Regiment, cared for the wounded soldiers with the assistance of Mrs. Harrison, a hospital matron. Mrs. Harrison was described as "*....Kind and attentive to all, particularly the Floridians.*"

Meanwhile back in the area of Dallas, the Brigade still faced light skirmishing and on May 30th, a Florida squad killed Sergeant Barnes of the 26th Illinois Infantry Regiment. The next day a detail of Floridians recovered Barnes' body and gave it a "*....proper burial.*" On June 1st, two 1st Florida Cavalrymen, [*Sergts. Sparkman and Ward* according to Washington Ive's letters], found the bodies of Lt. Kilpatrick and Sergeant John Burnsed from Company D of the Florida Cavalry. Captain Footman ordered a burial detail to take care of the bodies. The Regiment then moved to New Hope Church and was held in reserve to await orders.

In the middle of a thunderstorm, on June 2nd, the Floridians pulled out of New Hope Church and marched eight miles northeast on a road that became so muddy that they had to hold up in some woods. They tried to erect some breastworks in the heavy rain, but the area was so low that it was soon flooded.

Sherman, after giving up his operations around Dallas, had turned his army toward the railhead at Allatoona Pass. This had not gone unnoticed by General Johnston, he immediately began moving his Confederates to block the Yankees. The Florida Brigade was moved to Ackworth where they immediately engaged a moderate enemy force. The Floridians were then shifted with Bate's Division to Pine Mountain where they established a *"decent fortification of logs."* On June 10th, the Federals opened up on the right and subjected the Floridians to heavy shelling. During a lull in the fighting, Private Laton Sowell of the 4th Florida, was killed while trying to fill his canteen from a nearby mountain stream.

The fog and smoke hung heavy over the mountain, rain was constant, but the weather did not deter the several Union batteries of parrot guns from hitting the Florida Brigade's works. The enemy guns, only about a mile away, kept up a constant harassment of the Floridia regiments. Then on June 14th, the Union forces launched a full attack against the Confederates and attempted to drive a wedge into their line. Private Hutto Braddock was hit in the arm as his fellow Rebels held their ground against the advancing Yankees. At some point, Confederate Major General Polk was killed just behind the Florida Brigade's line. This fight ended with the Federals being thrown back, but leaving the Rebels too exposed to remain in position. That night, the Florida Brigade pulled back with Bate's Division and was moved to a better position east of Mud Creek. According to a New York newspaper article, one of Bate's soldiers, quite possibly a Floridian, had left an angry note pinned to a tree with a broken ramrod, which read, *"You Yankee Sons of Bitches killed our old General Polk."*

On June 15th, the 1st Cavalry and 4th Florida Infantry were placed in reserve in case they were needed to support Walker's Division. By the end of the day, Sherman had gained control of Lost Mountain and was focusing his attention on making Kennesaw Mountain the centerpiece on his table of battle. The Florida Brigade was immediately transferred to near Kennesaw and held in reserve for Cleburne's Division. In the meantime, the Federals had penetrated a weak point in the line between Hardee's and Loring's Confederates. The Floridians were then moved back in the direction of Lost Mountain as Johnston began shifting his lines toward Kennesaw Mountain. It began raining hard over the hills as heavy cannon fire bombarded positions all around Kennesaw Mountain. For the next few days, in a constant down pour of rain, the Floridians exchanged fire with the Yankees. On June 20th, the Floridians held a picket line despite a persistent wrath from Yankee cannons. Sergeant Wharton of the 4th Florida and Private Smith of the 1st Florida Cavalry, were both killed. The Union army, it seemed, had unleashed all of their might against the Rebels. The barrage of cannon balls smashed the Floridian breastworks throwing rails and mud all over the men. Twenty-two year old Private David Roberts, of Company C, was killed while seeking cover from fragments of exploding shells. The Federals succeeded in driving the Rebels from their works, but the Floridians were stubborn and soon reclaimed their ground.

The rains came heavy on June 21st, along with a deadly showering of 500 Union cannon balls that cleared the way for another Yankee charge against the Florida Brigade's entrenchments. The Floridians fought hard, but soon had to give up and pull back. Two days later the rain stopped and the warm Georgia sun began baking the bloody battleground. The 1st

Cavalry and 4th Infantry were detached and sent forward to fight from rifle pits closer to the Union battle line. Although many had faulty rifles, the Florida men fought gallantly and successfully managed to throw back a strong infantry assault.

On June 25th, things were fairly quiet on Kennesaw Mountain, only a few guns were fired just to remind the Rebels that the Yankees were still holding their ground. Lt. Daniel B. Knight, who had escaped following his capture at Dallas, had found his way back to the Regiment. During the war, Lt. Knight was captured by the Yankees on three different occasions and each time he managed to escape and return to the Regiment.

On June 26th, the Florida Brigade was sent to support Maurey's Brigade under Cheatham's Division. That night, all Florida soldiers having unserviceable weapons, were issued new Enfield rifles. The Brigade then moved two miles north and was held in reserve for Maurey's Brigade. The next morning, at eight o'clock sharp, the bluecoated enemy let out war yelps as they launched a determined charge against Cheatham's Confederates. The Yankees attacked with a force five lines deep. The Florida Brigade was rushed forward to assist Cheatham's men, but by the time they arrived the Yankees had already been turned back. An hour later, about nine-thirty, Sherman's army opened an inferno of rifle fire along a ten mile front. The air was thick with smoke and shell as the 1st Florida Cavalry and 4th Florida Infantry were moved at double quick to take up the slack between the Burnt Hickory and Dallas roads. During this movement, one squad was foolishly halted in full view of the enemy, which needlessly resulted in Private Sam Herrod being shot in the head. Just as Herrod fell dead on the Georgia clay, another round hit William Morgan in the arm. Washington Ives was close by and witnessed the tragic fate of his comrades and later recorded the event in his journal. The Florida troops had arrived too late to participate in the main action. That night they kept close watch over the Yankees while other Confederate units threw fire balls at the enemy to keep them from digging trenches under the cover of darkness. The 1st Florida Cavalry soldiers, confined to rifle pits, found no sleep that night, being kept awake by sporadic booming of Union guns high up on the mountain.

June 28th was a quiet, but extremely hot day, and the sun was swelling the Union dead that were still laying unclaimed on the battlefield. Early the next morning the Rebels saw a white flag being waved from the Union side. The Yanks wanted a cease fire so that they could gather and bury their dead. A brief truce was agreed upon and the Florida Rebels watched as over 200 Union soldiers crawled out of their holes to search the field for their wounded and dead. A few of the Florida soldiers went over and talked with the Yankees. It was a strange scene, an interlude in the horror of combat which allowed a brief, but friendly encounter between foes. The short armistice lasted until late afternoon, after which, the two sides returned to their mortal roles as enemies.

That night the rains came again as the fighting intensified along the Florida Brigade's front. The darkness was streaked with fire, Sam Nerod, of Company A, 1st Cavalry, was the first to die, Private Morgan, of Company F, and Private Willis of the 4th Florida, both fell wounded in the mud. The next morning, the Yankees opened the day with intense rifle fire killing Sam Ward, of Company A. The rains came down all day as the Floridians fought to hold their muddy place, but it soon became evident that they would have to abandon their position. When darkness came, the Florida troops quietly pulled out of their works and marched three miles to a spot near a railroad. Here they began building fortifications, but by morning the Union guns were aimed at them again. With shot and shell falling on them, the Florida Brigade moved to Cheatham's Bend on the Chattahoochee and was immediately drawn into a fight at Nickajack Creek. During this affair, Privates Daniel Thomas, James Thompkins, and John Thomas, were all captured. Both Earle Davis and Temple Powell suffered wounds while in combat on the Chattahoochee line.

By July 5th, the Florida soldiers had dropped back four miles to the south. At this location they found well made entrenchments, which had been prepared by Black laborers loyal to the Confederacy. The 1st Cavalry and 4th Infantry troops were soon tormented by more shelling from Union guns. On the night of July 9th, General Johnston ordered all troops to withdraw across the Chattahoochee and to burn the bridges behind them. The Confederate army moved south of Peachtree Creek, where they formed a defensive line on high ground and rested.

The Rebels hoped to block, or at least delay, Sherman's advance at Peachtree Creek. If they were lucky, the Rebs might force the Yanks back against the Chattahoochee, where there were no fords and no immediate access to Union supply lines. But, if this plan failed, the Confederates still had the option of falling back to the refuge of pre-constructed earthworks around Atlanta.

July 10th was restful for the Floridians, except for a constant drizzle of rain and a few distant booms from cannons across the river. The next day the Florida soldiers moved their camp to higher ground. Captain Maxwell arrived with two months of back pay for some of the 1st Cavalry and 4th Florida men. The next few days were warm and overcast, with intermittent showers. There was hardly a dry spot, or person, in the camp, the ground was saturated and clothing was soaked. Dry firewood was nowhere to be found and rations were running low. One soldier, describing the ordeal, wrote, *"At least we had plenty of water."*

On July 17th, General Sherman's army began crossing the Chattahoochee in massive force. At the same time, General Johnston was being replaced by Lieutenant-General John Bell Hood as commander of the Army of Tennessee. The change of commanders dampened spirits in the Florida Brigade, they liked Joe Johnston, and thought of him as a *"soldier's general"*, but had little good to say about serving under the harshness of General Hood. Orders were immediately issued for the Florida Brigade to stand ready to march at a moments notice.

By the end of the next day, the Floridians had relocated two miles to the northwest and were quickly throwing up a fortification of pine logs. The rains had cleared out and the sun was beating down on the barren red earth around Atlanta. The Florida troops soon found themselves locked in a skirmish with the enemy. The 1st Florida Cavalry companies, with the 4th Florida troops, pressed forward into the enemy line but were soon forced back to the safety of their defensive works. They crouched behind their logs and stuck their rifles through the cracks, but the Yankee infantry passed by without a shot.

On the 20th, Hardee's Corps was moved about two miles east and in early afternoon threw a full frontal attack against the Federals. The Florida Brigade, on the right flank, never made contact with the enemy. Most of the fighting was met by the left flank of the corps. General Hood expressed dissatisfaction with the performance of Hardee's Corps, saying *"They did nothing more than skirmish with the enemy."* Hood seemed to base his criticism on Hardee's low casualty rate as compared to that of Stewart's and Cheatham's forces, both of which sustained high losses. The Confederates, after spending 5000 lives trying to stop Sherman at Peachtree Creek, were once again forced to pull back.

The next night, General Hood sent Hardee's Corps south, on a 15 mile forced march to hit McPherson's Federals in the flank. Bate's Division led the midnight march through the hot dusty streets of Atlanta. The Florida Brigade was in the front of the movement as they marched by the dimly lit windows of war ravaged homes. The tramping of hundreds of feet and creaking of wagons, brought Atlanta folks to their doors to watch the long procession of ragged soldiers. *"At first we thought the Yankees had done come to Atlanta,"* wrote one Atlanta woman, *"...then the captain told us they was our boys going to beat* [the enemy] *away from our door."* Once the Florida Brigade was south of town, they turned eastward along rural roads, parallel to the Georgia railroad, and aimed for McPherson's location. To the east the day was breaking behind Stone Mountain. The Florida troops arrived at their objective weary, dusty, and half starved for the want of rations. The 1st Cavalry and 4th Infantry, took up positions along a tree covered ridge near Bald Hill. They rested and talked about how much they disliked General Hood and how they wished Ol' Joe Johnston was still in command.

On July 22nd, Hardee's Corps, with the Florida Brigade, was ordered to strike McPherson's army in the flanks. This fight, in which the 1st Florida Cavalry served so gallantly, became famous as the Battle of Atlanta and is depicted today in the massive painting at the Cyclorama in Atlanta. General Hood, and his staff, watched the action from the second story of the James E. William's residence. This was a major engagement for the Floridians, they went into full battle against the enemy and suffered greatly. Cleburne's and Cheatham's Divisions succeeded in capturing Union breastworks. Bate's Division, with the Floridians, attacked and was pushed back by overwhelming fire. When the hot, bloody day came to an end, the Federals had lost 4,000 men, including General McPherson. Hardee's Corps had lost 7,500, but failed to halt the Union army. The Florida Brigade suffered numerous losses, among which were Privates Griffin, Handcock, James Hodges, and Francis A. Triay. Among the captured Floridians were, Stephen Jones, James Pickett, William Smith, and Privates Temple, Whittle, Ellinor, Patterson, Mock, Collins, and J. W. Wilder. These men were all listed as being from the 1st Florida Cavalry or 4th Florida Infantry regiments. Most were later released in a prisoner exchange at Rough and Ready, Georgia.

49.

Hood's Army of Tennessee began pulling back into the defenses around Atlanta while Sherman maneuvered to put the city under siege and clip its life lines to the south. The Florida Brigade was transferred with Bate's Division to the extreme west flank of the Confederate lines. The Florida soldiers were engaged in moderate combat on August 3rd, in which Privates William Townsend and Nelson Johnson were struck down by exploding shell fragments. The 1st Cavalry and 4th Infantry troops were then advanced to a mile in front of the main defenses, near Utoy Creek, as pickets for Bate's Division. Over the next four days, the 1st Cavalry and 4th Infantry were involved in almost constant battle. At Utoy Creek, Private James Quinn fell into Union hands and John Crews was hit in the leg by a Yankee ball. During the initial days of Sherman's stranglehold on the city of Atlanta, the Floridians fought constantly, day and night. They were eleven miles from Atlanta and less than a hundred yards from the enemy. There was no time to eat or sleep, and supplies, especially ammunition, were becoming critically low. One soldier remarked about the lack of food and sleep, *"We take either when we can git it--as the damn Yankees are in charge of both."*

In mid-August the Georgia sun was compounding their agony by keeping mouths parched and thirsty. Mark Nichols was hit in the forearm and had to be pulled off the line, and like other wounded, he would have to suffer the shortage of medical supplies.

On August 28th, the Floridians marched with Bate's Division from their fortifications north of Atlanta, to Rough and Ready, Georgia, on the Macon Railroad. They set up camp near the station and stood ready for combat, while other Confederate units maneuvered into position to fend off an expected attack. It was rumored that a large contingent of Federals were concentrating in the area and were getting ready to do battle. When the enemy failed to attack, the Florida Brigade was moved four miles to a mill at the head of the Flint River, where they worked through the night constructing protective works. They had expected an attack at sunrise the next morning. Although the enemy did push back a small Confederate mounted cavalry they presented no threat to the Floridians. That night the Florida Brigade was moved to Jonesboro. The combined strength of the 1st Cavalry and 4th Florida Infantry had dropped to only 120 men and their fighting spirit had been stretched beyond the breaking point.

Major Jacob A. Lash was in charge of the 1st Cavalry and 4th Infantry Consolidated Regiment at Jonesboro and was ordered to deploy the Regiment to a small winding stream where Union infantry were gathering. The Floridians deployed as skirmishers but never made contact with the enemy and were soon ordered to rejoin their brigade back at Jonesboro.

When they arrived at Jonesboro they found that the Yankees had already reached the outskirts of the town. Once again, the Florida Brigade was thrown into action as skirmishers and persuaded the enemy to fall back. The Floridians advanced and were soon engaged in a limited, but vicious struggle with a hard fighting Union infantry. The Florida soldiers made a daring charge across 500 yards of open field against the Federals. Private Isaac Varnes was in the front ranks, although he was weakened by sickness, he gallantly charged into a blaze of Yankee fire. Through the smoke and confusion, Lieutenant Francis Fleming saw Varnes get cut down on the field. Fleming ran to help, but Isaac Varnes had drawn his last breath. Fleming was injured and had to be helped back by one of the sergeants. Not far from where Varnes had fallen, Joe Ellinor was calling for help, he too had been brought down in the charge. Sam Hunt had made it across the open field only to be captured by an enemy squad. Lt. Andrew Hagen, of the 4th Florida, was knocked backwards when he was hit in the shoulder but continued to lead his troops until the finish. The Florida Brigade suffered seven wounded while trying to seek cover in rifle pits, which had been recently vacated by Kentucky troops. Under heavy fire, and using only their hands and tin pans, the Florida men dug trenches to connect the individual pits together. The Federals were soon dumping an artillery barrage on the Florida position. Most of the shelling was coming from a heavy battery of Napoleon guns that were bent on keeping the Rebels pinned down. Sherman, upon learning of the Confederate's inferior situation, made an attempt to surround Hardee's Corps. On September 1st, the Florida soldiers launched an unsuccessful assault against enemy breastworks which resulted in Privates Mulkey and Parker being killed. Privates Bryan and Padget, along with David Smith and John Matthews, were taken prisoner. A shell exploded near General Finley and killed his horse. Finley, although severely wounded by shrapnel, refused to be carried to the rear until all of his wounded *"Florida boys were recovered."* Overwhelmed by the artillery fire, the Floridians had no choice but to withdraw to the rear. Finley's Florida Brigade had entered their ordeal at Jonesboro with about 700 effective men and lost 120, either killed, wounded, or missing in action.

Meanwhile, General Hood was evacuating the main body of the Army of Tennessee from Atlanta. That night, Hardee, still under a threat of being surrounded by the Federals, began pulling his Confederate corps out of the Jonesboro area. General Finley, still agonizing with his wounds, barely escaped capture by riding out in the back of a commissary wagon. The Floridians, with Hardee's Corps, were among the last to withdraw from the fury of Jonesboro. Hardee's Confederates began moving toward Lovejoy's Station to link up with the rest of Hood's army, which was retreating out of Atlanta on the McDonough road.

Through the night, the Florida Brigade marched hastily away from Sherman's forces at Jonesboro. In the distance the sky was aglow over Atlanta; the remaining Rebels were destroying Confederate supplies to keep them out of Federal hands. At about 2 o'clock in the morning, the weary Florida men heard the distant explosions of eighty ammunition cars being blown up in the Atlanta railroad yards. It was the final signal that Atlanta now belonged to Sherman.

All corps of the Army of Tennessee were concentrated the next day at Lovejoy's Station. The Floridians began building defensive works, but were soon ordered to proceed to Bear Creek Station. By September 8th, the Florida Brigade was camped in the woods on the edge of McDonough road, northeast of Jonesboro. Lieutenant Francis P. Fleming took time to scribble a few lines to his Aunt Tilly, informing her that he had, "...*just received* [his] *shoes from Mr. Oakley, a very nice pair and good fit.*"

On September 10th, a brief truce was called to allow citizens to evacuate Atlanta. Pickets from the Florida Brigade guarded a section of McDonough road as escaping refugees marched out of the city. After testing the Confederate pickets with a few hit and miss skirmishes, the Federals soon withdrew inside Sherman's perimeter around Atlanta.

On September 16th, the Army of Tennessee troops were inspected by their superior officers and found to be in poor condition. The long campaign from Dalton to Atlanta, had taken a terrible toll. The men were short on everything, some had thrown away any excess equipment during the long, hot marches, selecting to keep only their shoes, britches, shirts, and weapons. Blankets were either lacking, or shot full of holes, some men were using pieces of carpet scraps for warmth and sleeping comfort. But General Hood offered little consideration to these conditions, he ordered the troops to have three days rations cooked and be ready to move at a moments notice. The Floridians knew that this usually meant the start of another major operation.

On September 18th, the Florida Brigade, under Bate's Division, was marched twenty miles on a rough clay road to Palmetto Station on the Atlanta and West Point Railroad. Here the Floridians completed a fortification which had been started by Cheatham's Division. Several of the Florida men, who had been captured by the Yankees at Jonesboro, had been released and had returned to the unit. Among these ex-prisoners was the color bearer of the 3rd Florida Infantry Regiment, who proudly arrived still carrying his regiment's flag.

The Army of Tennessee, or what was left of it, reorganized at Palmetto, Georgia. General Finley was furloughed with his injuries and left Brigadier General Robert Bullock in charge of the Florida Brigade. Bullock was still limping with a minor foot wound suffered at Utoy Creek. The troops rested until September 28th, when they were ordered to prepare for a movement against Sherman's rear, north of Atlanta. Bullock ordered the Floridians to prepare two days rations for the march.

Hood's army was critically weak, his meager 35,000 Confederates were no match against Sherman's superior force. But Hood believed that he could draw Sherman out of Atlanta by threatening the Union supply lines to the city. In late September, President Jefferson Davis visited the Army of Tennessee and approved General Hood's plan.

On the 29th the Army of Tennessee crossed the Chattahoochee River on a rickety pontoon bridge at Pace's Ferry and by the next day had reached a point eight miles north of Campbelton. The following day they began marching north of Atlanta, almost backtracking their previous Spring campaign from Dalton. By October, the Rebels were tearing up Sherman's rail and telegraph lines into Atlanta. During this campaign of destruction, the Florida Brigade tore up and twisted railroad tracks, burned trestles, and ripped down telegraph wires. They engaged in several fights with Yankee patrols guarding the Western and Atlantic Railroad.

The Confederates soon left the railroad line and began marching northwestward, but carefully avoided Rome, where there was a substantial Union garrison. Initially, as General Hood had hoped for, the Federals had pursued the Rebels. But Sherman became befuddled by Hood's unpredictable maneuvering and notified General Thomas in Tennessee, that the Confederates could be headed north, or into Alabama.

General Hood's forces crossed the Coosa River on October 10th, and were heading toward Union controlled Resaca. Along the march, the Southern soldiers made several strikes against railroads in a continuing effort to cripple the Federal life lines to Atlanta.

Upon reaching Resaca, General Hood attacked the Union garrison and demanded that the Federals relinquish their hold on the town. The Florida Brigade was ordered to dig a line of trenches and prepare for battle, but before they had finished the job, they were ordered to proceed to Dalton. At Resaca, Hood believed that the Yankees would simply vacate the town, but when they refused to yield to his threats, he simply marched the rest of his army off toward Dalton.

On the way to Dalton, the Army of Tenneesee struck several small Federal outposts, tore up tracks, and forced the surrender of the 17th Iowa Infantry at Tilton. At Dalton, the Florida regiments were ordered to take up battle positions near Tunnel Hill road, while the rest of the army surrounded the town. On October 13th, the Florida Brigade assisted in forcing out the Yankees and recapturing Dalton. From Dalton, the Confederates moved north, skirting Chickamauga, then turning southward down the Chattooga Valley into Alabama.

By October 19th, after marching 300 miles in three weeks, with Sherman on their tails, the Army of Tennessee settled in Gadsen, Alabama. General Sherman moved nearby and waited in place for two weeks keeping his eye on the Rebels. Convinced that the Confederates would probably head for Tennessee, he decided to let General Thomas deal with Hood. Sherman then moved his command back to Atlanta to begin planning his infamous march to the sea.

By the 26th, General Hood had relocated the Army of Tennessee close to Decatur, but after intelligence reports indicated that a Union garrison there was much too large for his comfort, he moved out for Tuscumbia.

A week later, the Florida Brigade was bivouaced with part of the army on the banks of the Tennessee River, near Florence. For nearly a month, they had been living on boiled greens, roasted peanuts, and sweet potatoes, enhanced with an occaisional piece of hard bread. At Florence, they received a meager issue of supplies, including two days ration of four biscuits per man, but no items of shelter or warm clothing.

In spite of the cold the men were enjoying their first rest since leaving Jonesboro Each morning a thick fog drifted in from the river and the chilled air was already hinting at another hateful winter. They built camp fires for warmth against the cold and rain, and calmly waited for their next orders. As usual, idle times generated gossip, and this time a rumor passed through the camp that the Floridians would be heading back to Atlanta to chase out Sherman. But that would not be the case, for General Hood was already working on a much different fate for the Army of Tennessee.

THE FIRST FLORIDA CAVALRY REGIMENT CARRIED SEVERAL DIFFERENT FLAGS DURING THE CIVIL WAR. NONE OF THE ORIGINAL FLAGS ARE KNOWN TO EXIST TODAY, ONLY SKETCHES REMAIN OF SOME OF THE REGIMENT'S COLORS.

TOP LEFT- SEVERAL VERSIONS OF THE ST. ANDREWS PATTERN WERE USED BY THE REGIMENT IN 1862 AND 1863. *TOP RIGHT-*A SOLDIER FROM COMPANY "H" SKETCHED THIS FLAG ON A POSTAL ENVELOPE. IT IS NOT CERTAIN IF THIS WAS BASED ON AN ACTUAL FLAG IN USE OR JUST THE SOLDIER'S OWN DESIGN.

ABOVE- THE 1864 COLORS OF THE COMBINED FIRST FLORIDA CAVALRY AND 4TH FLORIDA INFANTRY REGIMENTS. THIS FLAG WAS CAPTURED BY OHIO TROOPS DURING THE BATTLE OF MURFREESBORO.

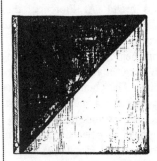 

THE REGIMENT CARRIED BOTH OF THE ABOVE FLAGS AT DIFFERENT TIMES IN 1864 AND 1865. *ABOVE LEFT-* IS FINLEY'S FLORIDA BRIGADE HQS FLAG, TWO TRIANGLES OF BLUE AND WHITE FORM A 54 X 54 IN. SQUARE. *ABOVE RIGHT-*THE HARDEE PATTERN, WHITE ON A BLUE FIELD, 36 X 58 IN.

Confederate artillerymen pulling back their guns on top of
Missionary Ridge as the Florida soldiers are overwhelmed by attacking
Federals down below. From a 1863 illustration in Harper's Weekly.

Confederates call a cease fire during the Battle of Kennesaw Mountain
to allow Federal infantrymen to recover their dead and wounded.
From a drawing by Alfred.R. Waud. Courtesy of Library of Congress.

**GEN. WILLIAM.G. M. DAVIS
THE REGIMENT'S FOUNDER
AND FIRST COMMANDER.**
Florida State Library

**PRIVATE WALTER PARKER OF COMPANY H,
DIED OF DISEASE AT CHATTANOOGA, MAY 1862.**
National Archives

**THE FLORIDA MONUMENT AT THE CHICKAMAUGA
NATIONAL MILITARY PARK**. Photographed by Charlie Carlson.

"Stand firmly by your cannon,
Let ball and grape-shot fly,
And trust in God and Davis,
But keep your powder dry."

Sold by Alpheus Bolling, Yorktown, Va.

Confederate States of America,

ABOVE: A patriotic letterhead from a Florida soldier's souvenir stationery. Writing materials were scarce for the few soldiers who could read and write, letters still flowed regularly between the troops and Florida.

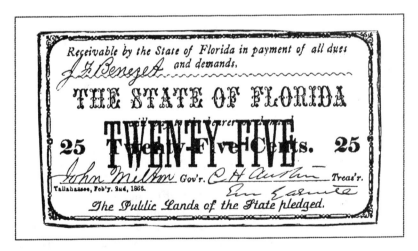

Receivable by the State of Florida in payment of all dues and demands,

THE STATE OF FLORIDA

25 TWENTY-FIVE 25
Twenty-Five Cents.

John Milton Gov'r. C. H. Austin Treas'r.

Tallahassee, Feb'y. 2nd, 1863.

The Public Lands of the State pledged.

ABOVE: A twenty-five cent note issued by the State of Florida. Fractional currency like this was issued in 1863 to relieve the shortage of change bills and to raise needed funds for the construction a Confederate gunboat. These low denomination notes were nicknamed "gunboat money."

CHAPTER SIX

THE FRANKLIN-NASHVILLE CAMPAIGN

Out of what may have been desperation, General John Bell Hood came up with a plan that would spearhead his Army of Tennessee straight into the heart of enemy territory. He would move his entire command through Tennessee and Kentucky, all the way to the Ohio River, where he would turn eastward and join up with Robert E. Lee's army in Virginia. Hood's idea was, that by linking up with Lee, the two armies could defeat Grant. Hood, however, failed to take into account the manpower and logistics necessary to pull off this strategy. Furthermore, General Hood had never consulted his superior, General Beauregard, the theater commander, nor had he submitted his plan to President Davis. Thus, Hood, acting on his own authority, began a careless campaign that would all but destroy the already battered Army of Tennessee.

On the morning of November 19th, 1864, Hood's army began their move into Tennessee, but heavy rains had rivers overflowing their banks and the roads were axle deep with mud. General Stewart's Corps, the first to take up the march, was held up by the high waters of the Tennessee River, which had also slowed the progress of the supply wagons. After much difficulty, Stewart's command made it across the river to the Lawrenceburg road. Lee's Corps followed next and bivouaced the first night between the Lawrenceburg and Waynesborough roads. Before sunrise, on the 21st, the Florida Brigade, [still referred to as Finley's Brigade], a component of Bate's Division, packed up and moved out of Florence with Cheatham's Corps. They crossed the river on flat boats and then marched along the Waynesborough road toward Columbia. After covering about eighteen miles, the Florida regiments made camp about a mile from the intersection of the Natchez and Waynesborough roads. The next day they made another eighteen miles and camped with Bate's Division near Furnace No. 96, four miles north of Waynesborough, on the Mount Pleasant road. On the 24th, they reached within twelve miles of Henryville and bivouaced next to Lee's Corps. On the 26th, Cheatham's Corps, with the Florida regiments, trailed behind Lee's Corps to Columbia. They immediately took up battle positions around Columbia with the Florida regiments situated between the Pulaski, Columbia, and Mount Pleasant roads. On the 27th, Cheatham ordered his forces across the Pulaski Pike and extended their lines from that point to the Duck River. Stewart then moved his Confederates into position beyond Cheatham just as the Florida Brigade made contact with the enemy. The shooting lasted until the edge of dark at which time the enemy gave up their claim to Columbia and began pulling out.

The next morning, at daybreak, the Confederates moved in and secured the town. There were reports, received by Hood's headquarters, of soldiers stealing and ransacking property. This prompted orders to be issued prohibiting plundering of private or public property. The Florida soldiers were not participants in the looting, as they had remained camped on the outskirts of town with Bate's Division.

General Bate received orders to move his division across the Duck River, about four miles above Columbia, and proceed to Spring Hill. Upon reaching their objective, Bate's forces commenced to form a line of battle against a substantial Yankee element at Spring Hill. The Florida regiments were placed in the left wing of this line and instructed to push forward against the Union forces holding the turnpike. Under heavy musket fire, mixed with light artillery shelling, the Floridians managed to advance about a mile by nightfall. That evening the Florida soldiers tried to take turns sleeping, but it was too cold and the warmth of a fire was prohibited by the closeness of the enemy. Then, to make conditions worse, in the dead of night, the Florida men were repositioned to within two hundred yards of the enemy. *"You could have throwed a rock and hit one,"* recalled a veteran many years later. In the process of moving up to the Federal lines, the Rebels had drawn some heavy rounds of fire. Union artillery soon began throwing a barrage at the Floridians, resulting in John Beach being wounded in a spray of shrapnel. When daylight came, the Confederates found that the enemy had pulled out of the area. With no Yankees in sight, a few of the Florida soldiers built fires and warmed themselves until orders came to prepare for the next march.

On November 29th, Colonel Robert Bullock, the Florida Brigade commander, was promoted to brigadier general. Bullock, 37 years old, was originally from North Carolina, but had grown up in Marion County. He had served as captain of a dragoon company during the last Seminole War. When the Civil War broke out, he joined the 7th Florida Infantry and rose through the ranks to colonel. He had been among the officers captured at Missionary Ridge and was a prisoner of war at Johnson's Island until he was exchanged in March 1864. He rejoined the Florida Brigade at Resaca and replaced Finley as brigade commander in 1864.

On the morning of the 30th, the Florida Brigade was in motion again, marching in the rear of Cheatham's Corps on the Franklin turnpike. The Confederates were directing their movement toward the backside of Winston's Hill, about three miles from Franklin, Tennessee. Here they prepared to do battle, but in mid-afternoon were ordered to move up to a line paralleling Carter creek. General Bate linked his lines at Carter creek with Jackson's and Tyler's brigades, behind which was held the Florida regiments for backup support. In this configuration the Rebels moved forward, beyond the creek and across an open plain. Although exposed to enemy fire, the Southerners successfully drove back the enemy. Under a furious fire, the 1st Florida Cavalry and 4th Infantry Consolidated Regiment was called forward and pushed their way past the Bostick homestead and successfully reached the Carter creek turnpike. They immediately turned left and went up against a strong force of Union infantry, but were soon overwhelmed and had to pull back. The Yankees were holding well constructed breastworks on an elevation which commanded a full view of the Rebel's charge. During the withdrawal, Levi Pearce was killed and John Crews was hit in the back. Private Harrison Starratt fell wounded on the field and had to be pulled to safety. Lieutenant

Colonel Badger was hit three times while commanding the 1st Cavalry and 4th Florida regiment. He gallantly remained with his men until his third wound forced him to the rear. Union batteries continued to pound the Floridians until midnight, but minor skirmishing continued until three in the morning when the Yankees began abandoning their positions. Colonel Badger was transferred to a field hospital leaving Captain George R. Langford in charge of the 1st Cavalry and 4th Florida Infantry Consolidated Regiment. The 25 year old Langford, from Hamilton County, Florida, had previously commanded Company F of the 4th Florida and is believed to have been the Regiment's only officer not captured at the bottom of Missionary Ridge.

Cheatham's Corps pulled away from Franklin on the morning of December 2nd and commenced a march toward Nashville. The coldness was becoming increasingly unbearable to the Florida men, most of whom were still without warm clothing and decent foot gear. The Florida troops, with Cheatham's Corps, trudged along the frozen muddy road in the rear of Lee's and Stewart's corps while General Forrest's cavalry rode out to protect the flanks of the column. During the march, Bate's Division, with the Florida Brigade and a battery of artillery, was detached from the main army and sent to Murfreesboro, a strategic Union supply and transportation point. Their purpose was to destroy the Murfreesboro to Nashville railroad. The 1st Cavalry and 4th Florida Regiment was assigned to the task of burning bridges and attacking blockhouses guarding the Nashville and Chattanooga Railroad. But Bate's entire force only numbered about 1600 men against an estimated 6,000 to 10,000 enemy troops in the area. When General Hood learned of the enemy's superior numbers, he directed Forrest's cavalry to reinforce Bate's expedition. The Florida Brigade, while enroute to the trestle at Overall Creek, about five miles from Murfreesboro, encountered a sizable enemy force. The Floridians successfully pushed their opponents aside and continued on with Bate's Division. The Florida Brigade was with Bate's Division on December 4th, in an attack on Blockhouse No. 7, which guarded the Overall Creek railroad trestle. Although the Rebels had made a vigorous attempt to take their objective, they were repulsed by a strong opposition. General Bullock was then ordered to have his Florida Brigade form a line of observation along Overall Creek. Colonel Kenan, commanding the 6th Florida, was instructed to hold his troops in the rear to guard the wagon train. The next day, the enemy made an appearance on the opposite side of the creek, but were persuaded to leave by a few well placed Rebel cannon balls. The Yankees pulled back, out of sight, but did not go far. That afternoon they returned, heavily reinforced with fresh infantry and artillery. The Federals quickly moved a skirmish line down to the creek where, at the edge of dark, they opened a vicious offensive against the Florida position. General Bullock was wounded in the initial attack when the Floridians were overwhelmed by superior firepower. Although greatly outnumbered, the Florida soldiers did not yield easily and stood their ground as best they could. Lt. Ira McCollum caught a bullet in his leg and struggled to find safe cover as Privates Horn and Appel fell captive to a Yankee squad. Jackson's Confederate brigade was not far away and swiftly responded to the Floridian's situation. Jackson's troops saved the Florida soldiers by pushing the enemy back across the creek. When the fighting was over, the Rebels had lost 15 killed, 59 wounded, and at least 13 missing and presumed captured. General Bullock, having only worn his new rank for a week, had suffered severe wounds and was now permanently out of the war. General Bate described him, and the other officers, as having *"heroic courage, both through good and evil fortune, always executing orders with zeal and alacrity."*

Major Jacob Alexander Lash, of the 4th Florida, was appointed to take General Bullock's place as commander of the Florida Brigade. Major Lash, 35 years old, was from Madison, Florida. He had joined Company C of the 4th Florida in 1861 as a Lieutenant and had participated with the regiment through all of its campaigns. He had served gallantly in battle as a company commander and as the regimental field officer. Following his promotion to major in April 1863, Jacob Lash soon found himself in command of the 4th Florida Infantry Regiment.

On December 5th, General Forrest divided the Confederate expedition into two columns and moved against the Union blockhouses at Read's Branch, Stewart's Creek, and Smyrna. Each of these blockhouses guarded a railroad trestle, all of which were put to the Confederate torch. Following this operation, General Forrest sent a dispatch to Hood's headquarters, reporting the capture of *"...the blockhouse and fort at La Vergne, with commissary stores, 100 prisoners, 2 pieces of artillery, 100 small arms and ammunition, 20 wagons, and some teams, and that General Bate had burned three blockhouses."*

After having caused considerable damage to a portion of the rail line, the Florida Brigade, under Major Lash, was sent forward, as close as possible, to the Union defenses surrounding Murfreesboro. On the 7th, the Florida troops were moved down the Wilkinson road as an extension of Palmar's Brigade. They soon found themselves facing a significant enemy force on the west bank of Stone's River. The 1st Cavalry and 4th Florida were then moved to the point where the Wilkinson road crossed Overall Creek. Major Lash ordered his men to immediately construct temporary defensive works of logs and rails. They were still piling up logs when the enemy struck with a full force attack, driving the Floridians, along with Palmer's Brigade, from their half finished fortifications. After running the Rebels out, the Yankees moved in and occupied the vacated works. In this affair, Private Jacob Dykes, of the 4th Florida, was captured. Strangely enough, this was the second time that Dykes had been captured at Murfreesboro. Two years earlier, during the first operations at Murfreesboro, Dykes had been captured and was later released in a prisoner exchange in 1863. But this time Dykes had plenty of comrades with him, Privates Fillingin, Harden, Herndon, Conner, Robert Horn, Bennett Osteen, James Braddock, Sam Crews, Corporals Scott and Hunter, had all been taken prisoner. John Weeks suffered a leg wound but had evaded capture along with John Vinzant, who had been shot through both legs. Many of the Confederates, including some Floridians, broke ranks and ran, causing disorder on the Southern side. Both Generals Forrest and Bate could not stop the rout which left the Florida Brigade scattered and confused. Most demoralizing was the capture of Sergeant Bryon, the color bearer for the consolidated 1st Cavalry and 4th Florida Regiment. Bryon was captured, along with the regimental flag, by the 174th Ohio Infantry Regiment. [Note: The Ohio Infantry kept the flag and later, after the war, donated it to the Ohio Historical Society. The colors were retained in Ohio for 107 years, then in 1971, the Ohio Historical Society made arrangements to return the flag to the State of Florida. To appropriately receive the colors, a state official was sent to Columbus, Ohio, to accept the flag on the behalf of the people of Florida. However, after the Florida representative received the flag it mysteriously disappeared. According to the Museum of Florida History, a thorough, but unsuccessful search, was conducted to find the artifact, but no trace of the flag has ever been found. There are no records indicating that the flag is in any official collection, of course that does not rule out the possibility that it is in some private collection. The only description of the flag is an illustration drawn by Ohio artist Robert Needham. In all likelihood, the flag captured at Murfreesboro was the last regimental colors carried by the 1st Cavalry and 4th Florida Infantry Consolidated Regiment].

Following the devastation on the field at Murfreesboro, the Florida Brigade pulled well back into the woods. It was late at night before Major Lash could account for his men and begin reorganizing the brigade. A few never returned, some simply deserted, while others fell into enemy hands while trying to find their way back to the Brigade.

A few days later, Bate's Division, with the Florida regiments, was ordered back to their previous duty of tearing up railroad tracks. Progress was slow in consequence of the freezing weather. The poor Floridians, lacking warm clothing against the chill, had to endure heavy snow and freezing rain while carrying out their mission. General Bate, in the official record, describes the shoeless condition of his soldiers, *"....many of the men were barefooted; all were shod however when we left Florence. I pressed* [into service] *every pair of shoes which could be found for them, and in many instances the citizens gave them second-hand shoes, which partially supplied the demand."* In spite of the lack of clothing and footwear, the troops did have adequate rations at this time, the result of confiscated commissary supplies. In addition to the captured subsistence, Bate had put several grist mills into operation to help feed his troops.

During the time that Bate's Division was attached to General Forrest's command, they were involved in numerous operations that had successfully disrupted Union supply facilities and communication lines around the Murfreesboro area. Then an order came down from headquarters for Bate to rejoin his division to Cheatham's Corps, now cooperating with the main Army of Tennessee in operations against Nashville. On December 10th, a terrible ice storm broke over the ill prepared Confederate troops. It was in this frozen rain that the Florida soldiers made their march over sleeted roads to Nashville. General Bate reported that *"....the sleet and severe freezes had made the surface of the earth a sheet of ice."* At least a quarter of the men were still barefooted and suffered extreme frostbite. According to many accounts, from those who were there, the shoeless soldiers actually *"...left bloody footprints in the snow as they marched."*

The Florida Brigade arrived at Rains Hill, in front of Nashville, and hastily constructed a system of defensive works to the left of the Nolensville Turnpike. Here they remained, fighting the extreme cold and trying to survive their frozen state. Then on December 15th, another fierce winter storm struck the area and covered the Florida trenches with snow and ice. That same evening the Florida troops were ordered to move out of their works to join a battle in progress. In the ice cold darkness, the Florida men moved rapidly forward through a marshy field and were soon exposed to the sights of Yankee sharpshooters. The Florida regiments worked through the night digging trenches in the frozen ground and fortifying their position. The Florida Brigade was the center of Bate's battle line, on their left was Tyler's Brigade and on the right was Jackson's Brigade. To their immediate front was a series of hills occupied by Federal infantry and a little to the left sat a heavy battery of field guns, all aimed at the Florida troops. The movement of Confederate artillery was hampered by the thawing of cultivated fields, but Captain Beauregard managed to place his howitzer battery on a plateau directly behind the Florida position. From this location, Beauregard's guns could sweep the front and, hopefully, interfere with any Yankee advance.

Early the next morning, the Federals began their move by deploying masses of infantry against the Confederate lines and planting new gun emplacements as they advanced forward. The Union forces threw a hard infantry charge at the Florida Brigade. Captain Beauregard opened his field guns in a blaze of vengeance and managed to slow the onslaught. From their trenches the Florida troops held their ground and successfully repulsed the Federal attackers. But the inevitable was only delayed, the Yankees quickly responded with a fury of artillery that lasted a full day. Under the cannon barrage, the left wing of Bate's line gave way allowing Union infantry to pour in and chase the Rebels from their works. Meanwhile, the Florida soldiers, occupied with Yankee skirmishers, were still holding tight to their center position in Bate's line. There was hardly no support on their left, the 37th Georgia Infantry had already been wiped out and several regiments on the right had been driven back into a field in the rear. The Florida soldiers, having little choice, began pulling back and were among the last to leave the line. Major Lash, while directing his Floridians from the field, was captured by the enemy along with Generals Smith and Jackson. The Confederate regiments began falling to pieces, leaving the withdrawing troops scattered over the battlefield. Major Glover Ball, being the next Florida officer in rank, took charge of the Florida Brigade. The 30 year old Ball began his service in 1861 as a captain with the 1st Florida Infantry Regiment. He was promoted to major in 1862 and captured during the Kentucky campaign. In late 1862, he was released in a prisoner exchange and rejoined his former regiment as a field officer. Glover Ball now had the difficult duty of trying to keep the Florida Brigade together during its chaotic retreat from the field. The leadership had totally fallen apart within the Brigade; its few officers, and sergeants, were either missing, lost, wounded, or captured.

The Federals had given the Confederates a severe beating at Nashville and had sent them retreating in the falling snow, down the Franklin

Turnpike. This disorganized exodus continued well into the night. The Florida troops, half frozen, starved, and exhausted, reached Brentwood in the middle of the night. Unable to go any farther they rested and licked their wounds until the next day. At sunrise, Major Ball called upon his few remaining officers to conduct a roll call and to start reorganizing the regiments. Captain Langford began piecing the remnants of the 1st Cavalry and 4th Florida into a regiment again. Many of the Florida soldiers were still missing while others continued straggling in during the day.

The next day, the battered troops of the once grand Army of Tennessee pulled out and headed southward to Franklin. They reached Rutherford's Creek, south of Franklin, on December 18th, where the Florida regiments, with Bate's Division, set up a defensive perimeter and rested overnight. Early the next morning, a Federal force made a showing and challenged the Rebels to several skirmishes. Following this minor encounter, but still mindful of the Yankees, the Confederates resumed their journey and were soon crossing the Duck River. On the 21st, the Florida troops camped overnight on the banks of Richland Creek near Pulaski.

The long hard journey was leaving weary Rebels scattered all along the route. Some were too sick to march and simply fell to the wayside. Several of the Florida soldiers were captured while trying to catch up with their regiments. Private Henry Crews, suffering from bleeding wounds, along with fellow Floridian, Private Stephen Johnson, fell into enemy hands as they limped past Franklin. John Douberly and Fleming Walker met the same fate on Christmas day near Pulaski.

The main body of Hood's army had reached Bainbridge by Christmas night and held up there until a crossing could be made over the Tennessee River. The pioneer company went on ahead with the pontoon wagons and began laying a bridge over the river for the escaping army. The Florida Brigade was detailed, as part of Cheatham's Corps, to establish a defensive line at the bridge site. Their mission was to provide security while Hood's army crossed safely over the river. It took the ragged Army of Tennessee two full days to make it across the river. The Florida regiments, followed by a rear guard of cavalry, were among the last to cross over to the Alabama side. By the 28th, Hood's army was on the other side and the bridge was dismantled and loaded onto wagons.

In Alabama the Confederate column marched until they came to the Charleston and Memphis Railroad, at this point they took a westward turn for Burnsville, Mississippi. At Burnsville, Hood issued orders to each of his corps commanders, directing the further dispositions for each corps. Stewart's Corps was to remain temporarily at Burnsville, Lee's Corps was to proceed to Rienzi, and Cheatham's Corps, with the Florida Brigade, was ordered to Corinth, Mississippi. The Floridians moved out on the last day of 1864 and by January 1st had set up camp at Corinth. After remaining there for ten days, they were then transferred with Cheatham's Corps to Tupelo, where General Hood had established his army headquarters. The 1st Cavalry and 4th Florida began building shelters against the cold. Some of the Floridians were granted furloughs and a number of others were discharged due mainly to poor health.

Hood's campaign into Tennessee had been a disaster; it had drastically reduced the fighting ability of the Army of Tennessee and had severely demoralized its troops. Yet, John Bell Hood assumed little responsibility for his carelessness, instead he blamed his failed operation on everyone else, his superiors, subordinates, and even his poor fighting men. The enlisted men privately cussed Hood for leading them on a miserable campaign. The fighting spirit of this once great army now seemed broken beyond repair. One Floridian later wrote, *"We didn't expect any victory & got no victory, we just got froze half to death & most of the boys lost their will to go on."*

General Pierre G. T. Beauregard arrived in Tupelo on January 15, 1865, with orders to ship the Army of Tennessee to fight Sherman's invasion through the Carolinas. Beauregard was outraged to find Hood's command in such wretched condition. What he saw was battle beaten soldiers, starving and sick, huddled in the smoke of filthy camps trying to survive the worst winter that Dixie had seen in years. Most of the men were shoeless and clothed in mere rags and only a few had blankets to fight off the cold. A few surviving regimental flags, tattered and shot full of holes, marked each regiment's camp. Few regiments had enough men to make up a decent size company. Captains were put in charge of regiments and majors were commanding brigades. Captain Langford was still in charge of the 1st Cavalry and 4th Florida Regiment and Major Ball was still commanding what was left of the Florida Brigade. After observing the shameful state, General Beauregard described what he saw as *"a disorganized mob."* It was clear to him that General Hood had to be relieved of command and replaced with a new commander.

On January 23, 1865, John Bell Hood, at his own request, was relieved of his command. In the interim, Beauregard put Lieutenant General Richard Taylor in charge of the Army of Tennessee and ordered him to prepare the troops for transfer to the Carolinas. Taylor faced a tough job that was compounded with logistical problems. 3500 of his soldiers were furloughed, another 4000 had been sent down to reinforce Mobile. This left only 5000 available for the movement, of which about 1300 were without weapons. Only about half of the Floridians were armed but were severely short of ammunition. The Nashville disaster had left the army with few remaining supply wagons or ambulances, and barely any serviceable artillery pieces. One of the greatest concerns was the poor condition of the railroads between Mississippi and Carolina. There were several different track gauges, which would cause bottlenecks of troops and require switching to different trains along the route. There was a shortage of rail cars, and to add to problems, Sherman had ripped apart a good portion of railroad through Georgia. Somehow General Taylor was expected to overcome these obstacles and relocate the Army of Tennessee across country for one final rally against Sherman. This overwhelming task would be remembered as one of the largest rail movements of the war.

CHAPTER 7

THE FADING ROAD TO VICTORY

In Savannah, Sherman's army was packing up and preparing to plow a furrow of destruction through the Carolinas. General Ulysses S. Grant planned to have Sherman's army link up with the forces of Butler and Meade for a strike against Robert E. Lee's Army of Northern Virginia. To insure that Sherman would have logistical access to coastal support, Grant had directed his Federals to take control of Wilmington and New Bern, North Carolina. After securing these places, the Yankees would eventually move inland and merge with Sherman. In late January, reinforcements of Schofield's Corps began arriving from the West. General Schofield was directed to take charge of the Union Department of North Carolina and to immediately organize his command for a rendezvous with Sherman in the vicinity of Goldsboro.

By February, General Sherman's massive army, consisting 60,000 troops in four corps, had left Savannah with 2,500 supply wagons and 600 ambulance wagons. The main opposition to Sherman's advance was Hardee's 8000 Confederates in the proximity of Port Royal Sound, a South Carolina militia of 3000, and about 1500 assorted Rebel cavalrymen. Over near Augusta, Generals Wheeler and G. W. Smith, stood ready with another 8,200 Southern troops. But these were small numbers; hardly enough to stand in Sherman's path, and the expected addition of the badly depleted Army of Tennessee would still only bring the available Confederate strength to about 25,000 troops.

The Army of Tennessee began its journey from Mississippi with Stevenson's Corps, followed by Cheatham's Corps with the Florida Brigade, and nearly a month later by Stewart's Corps. The Florida regiments loaded aboard rail cars on January 27th and pulled out of Tupelo that same afternoon. They traveled all night over the rough rails, down through Okolona to Meridian.

At Meridian, the soldiers changed to a waiting train and headed for Demopolis, Alabama, but shortly before crossing the Alabama border, the engine hit a faulty section of track and derailed. Although badly shaken, there were no serious injuries reported among the Floridians. The men climbed out of the cars, dusted themselves off, and camped beside the tracks until another train could be brought up the next day. They made it into Demopolis on the afternoon of the 30th, where they switched to another train that would take them to Selma. At midnight, about fifteen miles out of Selma, there was another delay when that train jumped the track. After two derailments, the troops finally reached Selma and were transferred to the "*Southern Republic*," a packet boat that would take them up the Alabama River to Montgomery. After a three day delay at Montgomery, the Florida Brigade was transported on a train of flat cars to Columbus, Georgia.

Some of the men and baggage, were shipped up the Chattahoochee to connect with the Atlanta and West Point Railroad. The main part of the

Brigade went from Columbus, on a route through Macon and Milledgeville, to the depot at Mayfield. Most of the trip was by rail, but due to poor conditions of the tracks, several miles between points, were marched on foot. For many of the Rebels, especially the Floridians, this was the closest that they had been to home since 1862. Needless to say, the temptation to run off to home resulted in a few desertions along the way. Others became too sick for the journey and were left in the care of private citizens, or when available, in local hospitals.

At Mayfield, the Florida regiments were packed into cattle cars on the Georgia Railroad and hauled to Camak Station, where, due to a difference in track gauge, they had to change to another train. The long rail journey finally came to an end on the night of February 10th, when Cheatham's Corps, with Florida Brigade, arrived in Augusta. The Florida troops unloaded and immediately marched across the Savannah river to the South Carolina side and set up camp for the night near the bridge. The next day, the Floridians were moved back to Augusta to assemble at the depot, with Bate's division. Some elements of Stevenson's Corps, which had arrived several days earlier, had already advanced into South Carolina. Other brigades were still strung out all the way back to Mississippi waiting for transportation.

As units of the Army of Tennessee continued arriving in Augusta, reports began filtering in that Sherman was threatening to move on Columbia. General Beauregard ordered Cheatham to move into South Carolina and start for Columbia. The Florida regiments crossed into South Carolina and marched twenty-one miles north to near Edgefield, where they went into bivouac at Bauskett's Mills. Two days later, after being joined by other regiments coming up from Augusta, they took up the march again. While in motion on the road to Columbia, Cheatham's scouts informed him that Union infantry was blocking his way. Cheatham reacted to this news by turning his column on a northwest detour around Columbia in the direction of the Saluda River.

Upon reaching the river at McNary's Ferry, Cheatham divided his corps between two crossing points. The artillery and Smith's Division, would cross at McNary's Ferry, and Bate's Division with the Florida troops, would cross three miles below at Holly's Ferry. By sunrise on Saturday, February 18th, the Rebels had completed their crossing and were on their way to Frog Level Station on the Greenville Railroad. To the east, Sherman had exited Columbia and was moving parallel to Cheatham on a direct course toward Cheraw, South Carolina.

When Cheatham's Corps arrived at Frog Level Station, they found a good quantity of commissary supplies. This brought a welcomed relief to the hungry bellies of the Florida soldiers, most of whom resembled racks of bones draped with rags. They were issued whatever could be cooked on the spot or stuffed into haversacks, with the excess being inventoried and prepared for shipment by rail.

From Frog Level Station, Cheatham's force moved on to Newberry and arrived at that point in a drenching rain. On the 23rd, they took the train from Newberry to Pomaria, South Carolina. They marched out of Pomaria on roads made muddy by two days of heavy rains. To the east, the same weather conditions were hampering Sherman's progression toward Cheraw. Soldiers on both sides, sank up to their ankles on the roads as teamsters plowed the supply wagons and heavy field pieces through the slippery, deep mud.

The Confederates rejoiced when word came that "Ol' Glorious Joe" Johnston had assumed command of all Southern troops in North Carolina. The Floridians were still irritated from that miserable campaign to Nashville and were glad to be rid of John Bell Hood. On the other hand, they held high admiration for Joe Johnston and felt that if anyone could put fire back into the Army of Tennessee it would be General Johnston. Some of the Florida boys still remembered how Johnston had requisitioned blankets and shoes for them at the start of the Atlanta Campaign. They trusted Joe Johnston's judgment and were willing to give him their best.

When the Florida Brigade, marching at the head of Cheatham's Corps, reached the banks of the Enoree River, they found it overflowing from the recent rains. There were no fording places, nor available ferries. With no other options, Cheatham ordered the men to start building rafts. Using the few tools that were available, the Rebels put together log rafts and after two days had ferried Cheatham's entire corps across the Enoree.

By Saturday, March 4th, the Florida Brigade had moved through Unionville, crossed the Broad River, and were bivouaced near Chester, South Carolina. About fifty miles due east, Sherman had taken control of Cheraw, a major rail terminal for Southern war supplies. Previously, Hardee's Rebels, after marching up from Charleston, had occupied Cheraw for four days. When General Hardee began feeling the pressure of the advancing Yankees, he began loading all the supplies that would fit into his wagons and prepared to move out. What the wagons could not haul, or his soldiers could not carry, was destroyed. Hardee's Corps left Cheraw to Sherman and headed out for Greensboro, but enroute he received orders redirecting him to Fayetteville, North Carolina. Confederate intelligence indicated that Sherman was aiming for Fayetteville with the ultimate objective of linking with Federal reinforcements at Goldsboro.

It was apparent to Joe Johnston that he would have to get the Army of Tennessee around Sherman. He directed the Army of Tennessee troops to proceed to Salisbury, then by way of Raleigh to concentrate with the Confederate forces at Smithfield, northeast of Fayetteville. However the movement would be slow due to the lack of rail cars. The few available cars were immediately sent down to Chester to begin transporting the various units of the Army of Tennessee as each arrived from Augusta. The Florida Brigade was loaded into four dilapidated boxcars on a train carrying Cheatham's Corps and transported up to Charlotte. At Charlotte, a difference in track gauge forced the troops to switch to different train. The Floridia men were crowded into boxcars and hauled up to Salisbury, where the rail yards soon became jammed with incoming troops. It seems that Johnston's headquarters had neglected to instruct the quartermaster in Raleigh to send trains for the arriving army. Most of the railroad cars were busy running supplies for the Army of Northern Virginia and it would take time to divert transportation to Salisbury. The Florida soldiers were stranded, but the delay was welcomed as an opportunity to catch a much needed rest and for tending to any ailments.

Two big problems were facing General Joe Johnston, Sherman was approaching from the south and Schofield's Federals were moving inland from the coast. There was no doubt that the two Union armies would connect at some point. General Johnston, on March 13th, made a decision to block Sherman's path, but to make this happen, he needed all Confederate forces concentrated at Smithfield. But the Army of Tennessee was still stranded, or strung out, from Salisbury half the way back to Augusta. General Johnston dispatched his acting chief of staff, General Beauregard, to Raleigh to get the trains rolling for the troops at Salisbury.

Meanwhile, over near Fayetteville, Sherman's columns were coming up fast. On March 15th, six miles from Averasboro, at Smith's Ferry, Hardee's small corps made a bold stand against Sherman's advance. The next night, in a hard rain, Hardee, realizing his limitations, withdrew toward Smithfield. He had paid the price in 500 Rebel casualties to cause the Yankees a loss of 700, which hardly put a dent in Sherman's numbers. Nevertheless, Hardee was satisfied that he had slowed the enemy's progress and gained a little precious time for the Confederates to organize their strategy. While on the road to Smithfield, Joe Wheeler's cavalry kept Hardee advised of Sherman's movement. It soon became apparent that the enemy was leaning in the direction of Bentonville.

Finally, after being stuck in Salisbury for six days, the Florida Brigade was on a train steaming its way through Raleigh enroute to Smithfield. On the afternoon of March 17th, the train chugged into the Smithfield depot. The Florida troops were unloaded and hurried off to a camp just north of town. Throughout the evening the buildup at Smithfield continued, as more trains arrived with units of the Army of Tennessee.

With most of the Army of Tennessee now concentrated at Smithfield, General Johnston, now in charge of all Confederate forces in the area, began reorganizing his command. He put General A.P.Stewart in charge of the Army of Tennessee, under which he attached all other available units, including Hardee's Corps. General Bate assumed command of Cheatham's Corps leaving Colonel Angus Daniel Kenan, commander of the Florida Brigade, in charge of Bate's Division. Kenan was another officer who had emerged from the enlisted ranks. He had joined the 6th Florida in March 1862 at Quincy, Florida, as a sergeant, and a month later was elected major. With Kenan taking over the division, Lieutenant-Colonel Elisha Mashburn became the new commander of the Florida Brigade. Mashburn had spent all of his service with the 3rd Florida Infantry and through attrition had been serving as second-in-command of the Florida Brigade. Captain Langford remained the commander of the 1st Florida Cavalry and 4th Florida Consolidated Regiment.

While the Confederate forces were being reorganized to confront Sherman in North Carolina, General Jesse J. Finley, the original commander of the Florida Brigade, having recovered from his wounds suffered in the Atlanta Campaign, was trying to rejoin his old brigade. Finley, coming up from Florida, had tried to reach Smithfield but could not get past Sherman's army. Unable to reach his compatriots, General Finley turned around and headed for Columbus, Georgia, where he joined General Howell Cobb's staff.

On the morning of March 18th, the Florida Brigade marched with Johnston's army twenty-one miles to a point near Bentonville. An observer noted, *"In spite of their ragged looks, our Southern boys marched along to whistling & singing."*

On Sunday, March 19th, Johnston ordered his forces to prepare battle lines two miles south of Bentonville to block the Union's approach to Goldsboro. The earth was still soggy from rains as the Rebels began digging entrenchments. They soon found themselves facing a challenge from Slocum's division in Sherman's advance. The Yankees moved forward with confidence, only to be met with a heavy volley from Rebel infantry concealed in a cluster of pine trees. The enemy fell back and began digging in. Slocum sent a dispatch to Sherman requesting reinforcements. General Stewart then formed the Army of Tennessee in two lines with Cheatham's Corps on the right end. The first line was ordered forward across an open field against the enemy hidden in the woods. The Federals opened with a blast of fire that sent the Rebels scrambling for cover. The first line was stalled by the Union resistence, they hugged the ground and took cover the best they could, but few were returning fire. General Bate, upon recognizing the situation, ordered the second Confederate line to advance forward. The second line, under Colonel Kenan, included the Florida Brigade. The first line was still holding to their cover, in ditches and behind logs, when General Hardee rode up and tried to wave the Rebels forward. Then to everyone's amazement, a color-bearer from the Florida Brigade emerged from the ranks and made a bold dash toward the enemy's position. With the First Florida colors flying, he came within fifty yards of the enemy. The Florida color-bearer's bravery was, *"....in such fine spirit and order as to reassure the first* [line] *and excite an emulation which caused the first line to move rapidly forward directly upon the* [enemy's] *works."*

With the Floridians at the head of the charge, the Confederates chased the Yankees out of their works and into the rear. The persistent Rebels, after punching a hole in the second Union line, successfully drove the foe from the field. The gallant and inspiring action by the Florida color-bearer remains one of the heroic features of the Battle of Bentonville. But this mild victory had not been without a price, Florida privates, Sam Hunt and Dixon Thomas, were both shot in the legs and had to be carried off the field. Considering the fierce fire that was poured on the Confederates, Hunt and Thomas were fortunate not to have been counted among the hundreds of dead and dying still littering the smoke clouded field.

The Southerners continued pushing at the Federal lines until they had driven the foe back to the Goldsboro road and into a swamp. That afternoon, General Hardee called for the Confederates to regroup on the north side of the Goldsboro road. At 4:30 P.M., the Florida Brigade having straightened its ranks, was positioned on the extreme right of the line. Bate's Division then launched a heavy frontal attack but was thrown back by strong resistance.

The pine woods had been hammered to splinters by showers of artillery rounds and the fields strewn with bodies from both sides. This was the scene in front of the Florida Brigade as they waited for the enemy's next move. Then Bate's line was hit in the left flank with volleys from charging Union infantry. *"Do your best!"* called out General Bate as he motioned his troops forward in repeated charges, perhaps two or three times, but never to gain an inch of ground. The Rebel line, thinned by casualties, was just too weak from exhaustion to face the mighty fire being delivered by Yankee muskets. During the assaults, Colonel Daniel Kenan, the former Florida Brigade commander, was brought down when his leg was shattered by an exploding artillery shell. He was promptly removed to the rear for amputation and sent on to the hospital at Charlotte. In his official report, Major-General Bate stated that the wounding of Colonel Kenan *"deprives the country of the services of a most gallant and efficient officer."*

At midnight, orders reached the Florida Brigade to disengage and retire to the rear with other elements of the army. This withdrawal was not easy, the Floridians, in a torrent of rain, had to return over the same open field they had fought across earlier that afternoon. In addition to being exposed to sharpshooters, the Floridians, in the darkness, were to recover any dead or wounded as they pulled back to the woods.

On Monday, the 20th, the 1st Cavalry and 4th Florida Regiment was situated on the extreme right of the Confederate line. General Bate was concerned about the weakness of the line. His battle front was stretched thin, about four feet between men, and there was no cavalry unit to protect his flanks. While the Floridians expected to be challenged by superior numbers, the opposite end of the line was attacked. Union infantry came out of the swamp like a lightening strike into the Confederate left. The Federals, in a bold charge, routed the Rebels from their rifle pits, but spared the Floridians on the right. The Florida troops could hear the commotion on the left as the battle went on all afternoon in a drizzle of rain. The Yankees had managed to move their cannons through the muddy field and were bombarding the left with solid shot. Anticipating the same fate as their comrades on the left, the Floridians waited at the ready, but to their relief, they were never threatened.

In early afternoon, the Federals successfully broke through the Confederate left and were pushing toward Bentonville and threatening to control the bridge across Mill Creek. The heavy rains had made the bridge strategic to the Rebels; it was their only crossing point over Mill Creek. Johnston tried to reverse the Yankee damage and called Hardee to drive back the enemy and fix the break in the Southern line. The two sides struggled all afternoon, finally Confederate cavalry and infantry were thrown against the Union force holding the Mill Creek bridge. Terry's Texas Rangers, in a classic cavalry assault, managed to send the Yankees off in a disorderly retreat. The Confederates then went about rearranging their lines and bringing up reinforcements from their reserves. The Rebel line changed completely, it now faced east, on a line beginning with the right at the Cole homestead and extending to Mill Creek.

General Johnston, expecting another hard assault against his left, pulled Bate's Division, with the Floridians, off the line at the Cole farm and sent them to reinforce the left end. As the Florida troops were moving in the rear to their new position, fighting erupted all along the Southern front. The Florida men moved at quick time to the left, however, once again, fate had spared them from the fighting. Although unknown at the time to the battle weary Floridians, this would be the last day of their final battle.

The firing and the rain continued deep into the night. The Florida soldiers, sheltered under a stand of blackjack and pines, were soaking wet and tired. They took turns trying to catnap on the wet pine straw, but could not close out the eerie moans coming from dying men still laying on the dark battlefield. Around two o'clock in the morning, a courier delivered orders for the Florida Brigade to begin withdrawing with the army on the muddy road through Bentonville and across the Mill Creek bridge. During the withdrawal, Rebel pickets were left in place to make the enemy think that the Confederates were still in position. The pickets were to be withdrawn before sunrise, however conflicting orders resulted in most of them becoming prisoners of the Yankees.

By early afternoon, the last elements of the Confederate army had crossed Hannah's Creek, well north of Bentonville, on the Smithfield road. When they were beyond range of the enemy, General Johnston posted a rear guard and halted the troops for a rest. On the 22nd, with a strong March wind blowing against their battle worn faces, the Rebels continued their move and reached Smithfield later that night. They bivouaced in their old campground while General Johnston and his staff, speculated on Sherman's next move.

On April 9th, General Johnston ordered another reorganization of the Army of Tennessee, which included the corps of Hardee, A. P. Stewart, S. D. Lee, Butler's division of infantry, Wheeler's and Hampton's cavalries. The Florida Brigade's ranks had been whittled down to about 200 men. The remnants of the 1st Florida Cavalry, the 1st, 3rd, 4th, 6th, and 7th Florida infantries were all combined to form a new regiment that was designated as the *Florida First Consolidated Infantry Regiment.* Lieutenant-Colonel Elisha Mashburn was appointed to command the new regiment. At this point, the Florida Brigade, still called Finley's Brigade, and its individual Florida regiments, all ceased to exist. The new Florida regiment was then assigned to General Smith's brigade, which was part of Brown's Division of Hardee's Corps.

Joe Johnston's army of 15,000, had gone into battle at Bentonville against an estimated 44,000 Federals. The Confederates had lost 224 killed, 1,770 wounded, and 600 missing or captured. At best, the Army of Tennessee now had an effective strength of about 14,000 and very few supplies. While the Confederate were trying to manage their shortages, Sherman's army was in Goldsboro being beefed up with troops and replenished with supplies.

On April 10th, as General Johnston began moving his army on the road to Raleigh, he received an urgent message that did not look good, General Robert E. Lee had surrendered to Grant at Appomattox. The news quickly spread through the ranks. General Johnston caught a train and went ahead to Raleigh to confer with President Jefferson Davis, who had just escaped the Federal advance on Richmond.

In the meantime, the Confederate troops, with Sherman now on their tails, pushed on through Raleigh and Chapel Hill, to the banks of the Haw River. That night the Florida Regiment made camp near the river, and then sat around their campfires, "*...reckoning that with General Lee giving up* [we knew] *the end had to be near."*

At daybreak, on the following Monday, the Florida troops broke camp and marched across the Haw with Brown's Division, fifteen miles to the banks of the Alamance River. Here they were instructed to make camp and to *"remain stationary until further notice."* It now seemed certain, their long struggle for a victorious conclusion was quickly fading.

General Johnston, after meeting with Jeff Davis, and with little options, decided to call for a temporary truce. Davis had wanted Johnston to escape with him, but the General ignored the order and began writing a letter of proposal to be sent to General Sherman.

By April 13th, Sherman had taken control Raleigh and was making plans to do the same at Salisbury, Asheboro, and Charlotte. The Florida troops, near the Alamance River, were told to *"be ready to march at a moments notice."* At the same time, Sherman had received Johnston's communiqué proposing a temporary suspension of hostilities and requesting a meeting of the two leaders.

Sherman agreed to meet with General Johnston at a small farm house on Hillsboro Road. The house, owned by James Bennitt, [often misspelled as Bennett] was midway between the two armies, about seven miles west of Durham's Station. On April 18th, Johnston and Sherman met on the dirt road in front of the Bennitt house. While still on horseback, they reached over and shook hands, then casually dismounted and went into the house. As soon as they were inside, General Sherman took a telegram from his coat pocket and handed it to General Johnston, saying, *"This came to me this morning from Washington."* Johnston scanned the brief message;

"President Lincoln has been assassinated."

The two officers wondered at what difficulties the assassination might create in their negotiations for peace. They sat down and began discussing Johnston's terms, not just for the military, but for the restoration of rights for all Southern people and amnesty for Jefferson Davis. Sherman tentatively agreed to most of Johnston's conditions, however, Sherman did not have the authority to negotiate any terms other than that which applied to military operations. When they were finished, the two generals agreed to meet again the following day. Sherman then returned to Raleigh to confer with his staff and Johnston went to General Hampton's headquarters near Hillsboro for consultation with his senior officers and to spend the night.

The next morning Sherman and Johnston met again at the Bennitt House. Sherman had bad news, the officials in Washington were rejecting Johnston's terms and were issuing orders for the Union army to reopen hostilities against the South. Joe Johnston immediately rode off to explain the situation to his staff.

Meanwhile, surrender gossip had made its way into the Florida camp, along with rumors that the Yankees were concentrating in all directions. Then came the news that the peace talks had failed and for the Floridians to stand ready to resume hostilities. Rumors began circulating that Lincoln's murder was inspiring fierce retaliation against the South. The Florida Regiment began battle preparations as Colonel Mashburn tried to sort out the facts from the rumors. On the 23rd, the Florida troops, expecting an encounter with the enemy, began marching to Greensboro, where, upon arriving, they were told not to make camp, but to standby and be ready to move out at a moments notice.

On April 24th, General U. S. Grant made an unannounced visit to Sherman's headquarters in Raleigh. Grant ordered Sherman to renegotiate the terms of surrender with Johnston. Sherman immediately sent a message to Johnston and scheduled another meeting for the 26th at the Bennitt House. In this final meeting, Johnston, having no other choices, agreed to the Union's terms, it would be a simple military surrender with no civil guarantees. The Confederate equipment, wagons, field pieces, and so on, would be inventoried and parked at a designated place in Goldsboro, North Carolina. Private horses, personal equipment, side arms, and baggage, could be retained by the Rebels. All other arms and military equipment were to be turned in to the respective state arsenals. All Confederate soldiers would be required to take an oath, *"not to bear arms against the Federal government,"* after which they would be legally paroled. The company commanders would be required to sign the paroles for their men. Union General Schofield was appointed to take charge of the surrender activities at Goldsboro.

At Greensboro, the Florida Regiment was placed in a "surrender camp" near the railroad to await their final disposition. The Florida soldiers present at Greensboro, were officially paroled on May 1st, 1865. The Regiment is recorded as *surrendering at Durham's Station*, since that is the nearest point to where Johnston had signed the surrender papers for all units of the Army of Tennessee. The Florida First Consolidated Infantry Regiment had 351 men on the rolls when it was surrendered. The final personnel strength for the First Florida Cavalry is difficult to determine, however, available documents suggest that only 35 men were present at surrender. There were, however, about 100 additional First Florida Cavalry soldiers carried on muster rolls, these included invalids on furlough, in hospitals, deserters, and those listed as missing or captured. At least a few other First Florida Cavalry soldiers were on detached duty and were not present at surrender. Those First Cavalry soldiers, who were not present at Goldsboro, were later paroled at various places in Florida.

During the first week of May 1865, the Florida men boarded a train for Charlotte. The train was overloaded with troops crammed into cars, riding on top, and *"....hanging on the sides of every car."* When the Florida troops reached Charlotte, they commenced their long march home by retracing their earlier trek through the Carolinas, back to Georgia.

In late May, probably about the 26th, the Florida Regiment was formed for their last muster near the Augusta depot. Colonel Mashburn stood in front of his depleted ranks, and after a few words of camaraderie, he said farewell. There are no recollections of what the colonel's parting words were, probably a mixture of praise, regrets, sadness, and relief. With a final salute, Mashburn dismissed the soldiers, and the Florida First Consolidated Regiment was officially disbanded.

The long struggle for Southern independence was over, but certainly not forgotten by those who had been tempered by its many battles.

The men gathered their few ragged possessions and began moving out on the long journey back to Florida, trying to push the war from their jaded minds with peaceful thoughts of home and family.

On May 20, 1865, the United States flag was raised over the state capitol, marking the beginning of reconstruction in Florida. Most of the ex-soldiers peacefully returned to their former rural livelihoods, as farmers, cowmen, or in the turpentine and timber trades. Others found their callings as entrepreneurs, lawyers, physicians, and civic leaders. But regardless of their fate, they were First Cavalry veterans, bound by a common thread of experiences that would be forever in their minds. There were no counselors for traumatic stress in those days, no help for war related disabilities, only a meager Confederate pension, which wasn't authorized until 1885.

William G. M. Davis, founder of the First Florida Cavalry, had resigned from the army in May 1862 and had moved to Richmond where he was active in the Confederate government's war effort. He purchased several ships which were used in running the blockade to bring supplies from England. Following the war, he opened a law office in Jacksonville and later served the law firm of Hughes, Denver, and Peck, in Washington D.C. He represented English cotton merchants before the U. S. Supreme Court in their claim against the United States for cotton it had destroyed during the war. At the age of 80, he retired from law practice and purchased an estate known as the "Dungeness," on Cumberland Island, Georgia. After the death of his first grandchild there, Davis sold the property to Andrew Carnegie and bought a plantation near Norfolk, Virginia. He died on March 11, 1900, at the home of his son, Captain Charles M. Davis, and according to his obituary, was the last living Confederate general.

Colonel George Troupe Maxwell became a physician in Tallahassee and in 1866 was elected to the state legislature. He later served as president of the Florida Medical Association. In 1888, he moved to Jacksonville and published several medical books. Dr. Maxwell is credited in medical history as being the first American doctor to view the vocal cords of a living subject.

William T. Stockton, after his release from Union prison, returned to his beloved wife, Julia, in Quincy. His health never fully recovered from the long months of incarceration as a prisoner of war at Johnson Island. William Stockton, at the age of 57, died on March 4, 1869.

Nobel Hull, former company captain, became a merchant engaging in business enterprises from Jacksonville to Sanford, and in 1877 was elected lieutenant-governor of Florida. In 1889, former 1st Cavalry lieutenant Francis P. Fleming, became the 15th governor of Florida. Martin Cox went into the lumber business and later became a county judge in Palatka. William Hall and Zachariah Mathers both enlisted in the U. S. army were shipped to the western frontier. John Vinzant became a school teacher in Lake City, but spent the rest of his life on crutches, and Frederick Merritt returned to Sumter County, where Merritt descendants still hold annual family reunions.

Aaron Guthrie ran a ferry boat on the St. Marks River and William Townsend became a blacksmith. Wiley Robson became a farmer in Lakeland and James C. Combs raised a family of 18 children. Samuel Goodbread and Arthur Roberts both served in the state legislature and James Fraser married Lizzie Crews and lived on a farm in Clay County.

William Hawkins raised cattle and told stories to his grandchildren about how the Yankees shot off his trigger finger in the Battle of Dallas. Jeremiah Walker settled in Basinger, down near Lake Okeechobee, where he was a rancher and justice of the peace, with a peculiar sideline of delivering babies.

Henry Berry, former private in Company D, opened a sawmill and turpentine business in Baker County and Harrison Starratt served several terms as a county commissioner in Duval County. Former sergeant-major Edmund Gillen became a lumber merchant, cattleman, and served as a tax collector in Jacksonville. John Brooks worked as a civil engineer and lived in Brunswick, Georgia.

There's a street in Plant City named in honor of William Collins, and on a street in Manatee County is the lone grave of James Vanderipe. In Ohio, at the old Camp Chase prison cemetery, on row 28, rests the remains of William G. Stokey. At the site of the Rock Island prison cemetery, in grave number 541, is the body of Tom Bracket. When Sergeant William Jackson was killed in battle, he left behind a widow with two children, and Daniel Mathis left three children for his wife to raise. George Wright was captured during the war, and is still missing in action. Like so many of their comrades, these Floridia soldiers never made it home.

By the 1920s, there were only 29 known veterans of the First Florida Cavalry still living. In 1936, Strother Gaines died in Oakhill, Florida, and was buried across the railroad tracks at the local cemetery.

When James Starling passed on in 1940, he left Henry Taylor Dowling as the last known surviving veteran of the Regiment. Dowling, who was a resident at the Georgia Confederate Soldiers Home, died on November 6th, 1948, at the age of 99.

The passing of Henry Dowling closed the final chapter of life for the valiant men of the First Florida Cavalry Regiment, dismounted, C.S.A.

THE FIRST FLORIDA CAVALRY REGIMENT C.S.A.
MEMORIAL MUSTER ROLL

NOTE: THE LISTED RANKS AND COMPANY ROLLS, ARE ACCORDING TO A SOURCE FROM A SPECIFIC DATE. RANKS VARIED DURING A SOLDIER'S SERVICE. MANY OF THE ENLISTED MEN LATER SERVED AS OFFICERS, AND SOME OF THE MEN SERVED IN MORE THAN ONE COMPANY.

HEADQUARTERS STAFF

William George Mackey Davis
George Troupe Maxwell
William Tennent Stockton
Thomas J. Shine
R.C.Williams
W.S.Harris
William Henry Pope
George Pinkney Wilson
Henry McCall Holmes
Elias E. Whitner
Thomas H. Maxwell
Robert L. Wiggins [Chaplain for 1st Cav.and 4th Infantry 1863]

COMPANY A

Capt. Arthur Roberts
Lt. Reuben H. Charles
Lt. James E. Young
Lt. William L. Jones
1st Sgt John F. Niblack
2nd Sgt William H. Carver
3rd Sgt William A. Marcum
4th Sgt Thomas L. Roberts
1st Cpl Lewis Willliam Rivers
2nd Cpl Kinchen T. Bell
3rd Cpl James L. Bryant
4th Cpl Green Berry Goodman
Company A Privates
William A. Adams
George D. Allen
Amon L. Barnes
George Blitch
William B. Boyd
Berry A. Brannen
James O. Brooks
John A. Brooks
John C. Brown
Edward Bryant
Ezekiel J. Bryant

Lorenzon Bryant
Rizan V. Bryant
William Bryant
George W. Burchett
Dawson E. L. Carleton
Lewis C. Carlton
Adam Carraway
William E. Carter
Amon L. Charles
Rupert Charles
W. L. Cone
John Nathan Cook
Martin Icabod Cox
William A. Cox
Columbus D. Craig
John L. Crawford
William S. Davis
Jacob S. Dexter
Jacob Jesse. Douberly
James Isaiah Dubose
Kinney D. Edge
Joseph P. Ellis
David L. Evers
William J. Feagle
Ignatious Griffin
John Griffin
Christopher C. Grisham
John Hair
Stanhope Harris
Pickins M. Harvard
William W. Harvard
William B. Harvey
John Wesley Herring
John L. Herrod
Samuel J. Herrod
Leroy F. Helton
J. S. Hogans
Robert James Horn
Micheal H. Horn
William F. Hunt

Nathan Haynes Hunter
Francis M. Ingraham
John A. Jackson
Daniel F. Jenkins
Nelson G. Johnson
Pinkney Jones
Irving G. Kinard
Shelton G. Kinnard
Wiley L. Koon [or Coon]
James M. Langston
Freeman Lee
Robert J. Legget
Rueben Levi Marcum
Church McCoy
Joseph McKay
Benjamin Franklin Meeks
William F. Morgan
William L. Moseley
Clinton Neal
H. W. Neal
Obediah Neal
Mark Nichols
Stephen W. Oats
George R. Ogden
Bennett D. Osteen
Paul C. Osteen
John E. Parramore
Henry Clay Parrish
Levi T. Pearce
John Simson Ponchier
James Powell
Temple Powell
William L. Powell
F. Roberts
George W. Roberts
Henry C. Roberts
Hezekiah L. R. Roberts
John D. Roberts
John F. Roberts
Robert Burnett Roberts
Joseph H. Robinson
Andrew Scott
Wilson A. Scott
William Lawrence Smith
John H. Tedder
Temp Tillis
Henry C. Tompkins
James T. Tompkins
William H. L. Townsend

John Vinzant Jr.
Isaac Waters
James W. White
William F. Williams
William W. Willis
James Soloman Witt
Jasper Hamilton Witt
Miles Melton Yeomans

COMPANY B

Capt. John G. Haddock
Capt. Isham M. Blake
Lt. Joseph N. Haddock
Lt. Crozier C. Jones
Lt. Daniel R. Howell
1st Sgt Drury Jones
2nd Sgt John W. Pickett
3rd Sgt John F. Lloyd
4th Sgt James Madison Price
1st Cpl Madison Higginbotham
2nd Cpl George W. Ford
3rd Cpl John Farliss
3rd Cpl William C. Darden
4th Cpl Samuel Russell

Company B Privates
Bradley G. Barnard
James T. Blue
James T. Bolton
Henry Edward Braddock
Hutto L. Braddock
James A. Braddock
John Spicer Braddock II
Joseph Braddock
William S. Braddock
Meredith E. Brock
John Brooks
John Brown
James D. Carmichael
Gill Charney
Abraham H. Colson
William Riley Conner
John G. Cook
Reuben Cottle
William M. Cox
George Riplett David
John W. David
Earle Davis
Jackson J. Davis
D. H. Dunn

74.

William C. Durrance
Jacob Saylor Geiger
Edmund W. Gillen
David Green
James H. Griffin
David G. Hagan
Jackson Hagin
Joseph Hagin
John A. Hall
Francis M. Hammond
James W. Hammond
Bourbon L. Higginbotham
Joseph H. Higginbotham
George W. Hogan
R. H. Holgerson
Nathaniel A.B. Howard
William Harrison Howell
Reuben J. Hughes
Jefferson F. Hunt
John M. Hunt
Nathaniel F. Johnson
Augustus Jones
John Hampton Jones
Stephen Jones
Wiley C. Jones
William Jones
George Kelly
Richard Lang
James B. Lloyd
William Henry Lloyd
Theodore Mathews
James McKendree
Mark L. Mckendree
James R. Musselwhite
D. J. Nettles
Henry Nettles
John Nettles
Wilson Nettles
Lewis Norton Jr.
Archibald T. S. Osteen
Ezekiel Osteen
James E. Pickett
Jacob Pope
John Richardson
John David Rollins
William W. Rollins
Azel Rowe
John E. Rowe
William Rowe

David D. Smith
John Smith
Harrison Starratt
Constant H. Stevens
David Stratton
Zachariah Summerall
Benjamin H. Tanner
Cornelius Tanner
Joshua B. Tanner
Daniel D. Thomas
Dixon Thomas
Eli Thomas
John J. Thomas
William Thomas
John C. Thompson
Isaac Tison
John Vickory
Edward J. Wainwright
M. Waskind
Bradshaw H. Webster
William H. West
Thadeus W. Wiles
Stephen W. Williamson
Burns Wilson
David B. Wilson
William Wilson
James A. Wingate
James H. Wingate
John M. Wingate
William H. Wingate
John M. Wright

COMPANY C

Capt. John A. Summerlin
Capt. T.P.Wall
Lt. William M. Saunders
Lt. Joseph J. Nickels
Lt. Jacob Johns
Lt. Daniel B. Knight
1st Sgt William Wilson
2nd Sgt James R. Knight
3rd Sgt Joshua E. Falana
4th Sgt Henry O. Silcox
1st Cpl. Calvin Livingston
2nd Cpl. James R. Houston
3rd Cpl. James H. Hardenbrook
4th Cpl. William B. Moore
Company C Privates
Thomas H. Arrick

John M. Beach
Joseph Beach
David Blackwelder
Minton E. Bloodsworth
John Booth
George Washington Branning
Amos Britt
William N. Brooker
Hezekiah Brown
Elisha W. Carter
Excellent C. Chalker
Benjamin L. Chandler
John W. Clark
William Collins
John M. C. Conway
Henry E. Dickerson
William J. Dickinson
Francis J. Dillaberry
John Dias
James Dyess
John Dyess
George R. Falana
Reuben Ford
William Ford
George W. Fouts
Albert G. Frasier
James Strother Gaines
James M. Geiger
Plen Geiger
Claiborn Ginan
Daniel Gunter
William Guthrey
George W. Haws
John Haws
Henry B. Hinson
Edward D. Hodges
Joseph B. Holder
Isaac Johns
Jeremiah Johns
Luke Johns
William Johnson
David Kellam
Thomas Kellam
Elijah Kersey
John Kite
Robert Edward Kite
William H. Knight
Emanuel Knowles
Henry Knowles

George W. Long
Joseph Long
John Mathews
William Edward Mathews
Patrick McCluskee
Barnabas McRae
Norman Harlow McRae
James C. Mobley
Clement F. Moseley
Wiley Nettles
Zachariah Owens
John Peacock
Henry Pelt
William T. Prevatt
James T. Quinn
William H. Register
David Roberts
Peter Rollins [or Rawlins]
Charles H. Rozier
Charles R. Rozier
James H. Rozier
Solomon J. Rozier
Henry Sapp
John D. Sapp
Thomas J. Shine
John Simpson
James Smith
Andrew J. Sparkman
Edward W. Speir
Joseph J.B.H. Swift
Simeon D. Swift
John P. Sylvestor
Cornelius Thomas
James M. Thomas
Adam Tison
William Tison
William P. Trantham
Thomas Underwood
Henry Ward
John W. Wilson
Josiah Wilson
Warren Wood
John Wright
William H. Wright

COMPANY D

Capt. John Harvey
Capt. John F. Pane
Capt. David Elwell Maxwell

Lt. Joseph Francis Pons
Lt. Francis Philip Fleming
Lt. Andreas B. Canova
Lt. James M. Burnsed
1st Sgt. Darling C. Prescott
2nd Sgt. Moses Blackwelder
3rd Sgt. John E. Burnsed
4th Sgt. Lewis C. Carlton
1st Cpl. William M. Driggers
2nd Cpl. James D. Hunter
3rd Cpl. Joseph Francis Haag
4th Cpl. Sebastian Genova

Company D Privates

William R. Alford
Thomas Barton
Nathaniel Beal
Berry Beasley
Hiram Beasley
William Beasley
Henry D. Berry
Duncan Bohannan
John D. Bohannan
Perry Browning
James Burnsed
James W. Burnsed
Phineas Burnsed
W. M. T. Byrd
Bartolo Casamana Canova
James Jackson Combs
William Combs
James Cosey
Samuel G. Crews
John C. Davis
Richard B. Davis
Benjamin C. Dobson
Berian M. Dowling
James R. Dowling
William Hampton Dowling
Aaron Driggers
Robert B. Dugger
William David Dukes
Frank Fai
Emanuel Falaney
John Falaney
Joseph Falaney
Thomas Falaney
James M. Fraser
William M. Garrett
Christie C. Gordon

Anson R. Green
Luther J. Green
William Green
Aaron Guthrie
Aaron Gwaltney
James A. Harvey
John W. Harvey
James M. Hodges
William Hull
Elisha Hunter
Henry Hunter
Wilson Jernigan
Jarvis Johns
Reuben H. Johns
Riley Johns
William B. Johns
Josiah Johnson
Stephen Johnson
Stephen S. Johnson
John Johns
Jeremiah Lee
Simeon Lee
William J. Lee
David Long
John H. Mathis
Henry Motes
William Motes
Hubert Natville
Henry Nowling Sr.
Noah Graham Osteen
James Benjamin Partin
Henry Philips
Riley W. Philips
Jacob Raulerson
Michael Rawls
Thomas B. Redding
William Rhoden
Jonathon Knight Roberts
Gomecindo Sallas
Sebastin Sebastin
William S. Scarborough
James T. Shaw
Jackson W. Smith
Harrison Starratt
William F. Sweat
Thomas R. Taylor
William Absolam Townsend
Francis A. Triay
John Valley

Andrew L. Varnes
Isaac Varnes
James I. Walker
Jeremiah Walker
Frederick Wells
Henry Wells
William J. Wells
Thomas E. Yarbour

COMPANY E

Capt. Charles F. Cone Sr.
Capt. John M. Footman
Lt. Wiley Lee Sr.
Lt. Richard F. Hart
Lt. Edmund M. Smith
Lt. Julian Betton
Lt. William B. North Crews
1st Sgt. David Bell
2nd Sgt. Robert Hayes
2nd Sgt. William S. Bugg
3rd Sgt. Columbus D. Craig
4th Sgt. Benjamin C. Jackson
1st Cpl. Thomas A. Walston
2nd Cpl. Charles M. Mitchell
3rd Cpl. Wiley Robson
4th Cpl. Jacob Wilson Brooks

Company E Privates

Thomas N. Bell
John Bennett
Foster C. Bethea
James W. Brever
Benjamin R. Bryan
Joseph H. Bryan
Nathaniel L. Bryan
John Burnett
Edward S. Butler
Eliga A. Butler
Antonio Cabiro
Harley G. Cason
William Washington Chapman
Charles W. Cheshire
James L. Cheshire Jr.
Henry Crews
John L. Crews
John N. Crews
Joseph Crews
Solomon B. Cribbs
Sampson Darrell
John Daugherty

Charles J. Davis
Lawson G. Davis
John Moses Dowling
John Durrance
Robert E. Ginn
John L. Guess
John D. Gulp
George Hair
George Hayes
Isaac Hines
Joseph S. Hogan
Lewis Hogan
John G. Humphreys
David Hunter
George W. Hunter
Jesse Hunter
Robert H. Hunter
James Middleton Jackson
Lewis A. Johnson
Moses Johnson
William R. Johnson
George W. Kelley
John C. Kite
Edward M. Lee
Joshua H. Lee
George M. Lewis
Sampson Lovell
Daniel M. Mathis
Hillard McInnis
James D. McKinney
Archie McKisic
Samuel E. Mobley
William Murdock Newman
John O'Donald
Isham Pagett
Joseph F. Polk
Owen C. Pope
Francis M. Register
David Roberts
John Henry Roberts
Patrick D. Roberts
James Robson
Daniel P. Saffold
John Shealds
William Sills
Hezekiah Smith
Jacob Smith
James T. Smith
David Stapleton

78.

George L. Stearns
Harvey E. Stearns
William E. Stearns
William G. Stokey
Sampson Tavell
Lewis L. Taylor
Edmund M. Thompson
Lem Turner
Edward Tynin
William W. Willis
Gideon Yelvington
Jesse Yelvington

COMPANY F

Capt. William M. Footman
Capt. Benjamin M. Burroughs
Lt. Richard B. Maxwell
Lt. Joseph J. Chaires
Lt. Joseph H. Sappington
1st Sgt. John Bradley MacLeod
2nd Sgt. James H. Lamb
3rd Sgt. John Parker
4th Sgt. David W. Scott
1st Cpl. John Sherrod
2nd Cpl. Stephen D. Bell
3rd Cpl. William S. Bugg
4th Cpl. James T. Benton

Company F Privates

Lewis D.H. Abrams
Elijah Andrews
Irvin Anderson
Thomas Ashley
Hartwell T. Ball
William J. Baxley
Thomas R. Bracket
Ball Burns
Michael Burns
John M. Coleman
William C. Collins
James A. Cook
Tobias W. Cook
Thomas N. Cox
Lanier C. Crafton
Allen B. Davis
Elijah Davis
Thomas F. Davis
John Alexander Durrance
Joseph D. Ellinor
Joshua H. Ellison

Levi Ellison
James W. Faulkner
John M. Footman
Thomas Newell Footman
James F. Gibson
James M. Giles
Stephen Godwin
William F. Gwaltney
Hazard Perry Hall
Oscar C. Hall
James C. Harrell
Morgan Harrell
James P. Harrell
Henry Alcy Hawk
John Wesley Hines
William A.J. Howard
Theoditus Hudnall
John M. Hurst
Theophilus H. Hurst
William M. Hurst
William Jackson
George W. Johnson
Milton Johnson
Newton Johnson
William M. Johnson
Thomas F. Joyner
William Kersey
James Irvin Kinsey
Thomas J. Lanier
Robert E. Lester
John F. Lynn
William N. Lynn
John G. Mathers
Henry Mattair
Willis B. Maynor
Franklin W. McDowell
William McDowell
Francis H. MacLeod
Amos H. Meeks
Franklin Miller
Burrell Mobley
Shadrick Newman
Hugh W. Nicholson
Nicholas M. Nicholson
Elijah Nix
John W. Oliver
E. W. Paley
Daniel Parker
Isaac A. Powell

John M. Raker
Virgil A. Renfroe
David Rives
David Sallis
Thomas J. Shine
David R. Shuler
Joseph Silva
Richard J. Singleton
Richard W. Slauter
Asa B. Smith
Edward Smith
William James Spencer
William M. Stafford
James C. Stephens
John B. Stokely
John E. Stokely
John W. Stokes
Melchezedec Thompson
George W. Tully
William C. Tully
Simon Turman
Henry W. Walker
Miles M. Wamack
David Whigham
John Winchester
Henry G. Woods
James Woods
Abram W. Youngblood

COMPANY G

Capt. William D. Clark
Capt. George Dewson
Lt. Samuel J. Kennard
Lt. Richard K. Taylor
Lt. James J. Weeks
Lt. Henry F. Horne
Lt. Stephen Weeks
1st Sgt. James J. Kennard
2nd Sgt. James W. Allen
3rd Sgt. George W. Register
4th Sgt. Jacob G. Stroble
5th Sgt. Robert Brown Weeks
1st Cpl. Jacob Kelley
2nd Cpl. Riley Moore
3rd Cpl. McCager Mobley
4th Cpl. Irvin Hamilton
Company G Privates
William Anderson
C. S. Avery

James A. Barker
Joseph H. Barry
William Franklin Barry
William M. Beale
James H. Boone
Allen Brown
Bartholamew C. Brown
William B. Brown
Rizan V. Bryant
John Call
Bartolomew C. Cason
Leroy Chesser
William W. Chesser
Joseph M. Christwell
George Cole
John H. Cole
Alfred Conner
Henry Conner
William H. Dinikins
John D. Dorman
Cornelius Drawdy
Luke Drawdy
Smith Dade Drawdy
John Dunaway
James M. Ennis
Matthew Ennis
Benjamin Arnold Fussell
William Henry Gaskins
Murdock G. Gillis
Harvey Godwin
Henry Hagan
Peter T. J. Hagan
John C. Hague
William Hall
Calvin Hamilton
Sherrod M. Hamilton
William W. Hester
Henry Hicks
E. T. Howell
John Allen Jackson
John O. Kelly
Jesse Lee
Daniel Lynn
William Lynn
[unk] McEnnis
David McGlon
James W. McRae
James Matteair
Frederick Lucius Merritt

Lucius M. Merritt
William Miller
Ransom Mobley
Jackson L. Moore
James Moore
Hezekiah Newberry
Alfred Nobles
John North
John Odom
Henry Pander
Richard Wilson Parker
William H. Paschall
Thomas J. Perry
Reuben Prevatt
Hardy Raulerson
James F. Register
James T. Reynolds
William Frank Reynolds
Job T. Richard
Harrison Roach
James S. Roberts
Francis X. Sanchez
John L. Sparkman
George W. Stanton
David L. Stroble
Henry G. Stewart
James E. Thomas
John Tyer
Edward J. Tyner
Richard W. Ward
George W. Weeks
Simeon S. Weeks
Daniel Weimer
Townsend Weimer
John Williams

COMPANY H

Capt. Noble A. Hull
Capt. Joseph H. Dupont
Lt. Joseph R. Haddock
Lt. Daniel C. Sanders
Lt. Nicholas Ware Eppes
Lt. William Edwards
Lt. James P. Morgan
1st Sgt. Meredith E. Brock
2nd Sgt Ira L. McCollum
3rd Sgt Henry H. Herring
4th Sgt. George W. Baker
1st. Cpl. Sinclair Demere

2nd Cpl. George W. Dupree
3rd Cpl. William B. Davenport
4th Cpl. Isaac J. Wiley
Company H Privates
Benjamin Bass
James H. Bozeman
Peter Bronson
David Cannon
Jackson Cannon
Madison Cannon
Samuel Cannon
James H. Corbin
John F. Coward
Jasper Curl
Jesse Curl Jr.
Jesse Curl Sr.
Joseph H. Dawson
Leonard Deese
Nathaniel M. Deese
William Deese
Sylvester Dempsy
Joseph A. Ellis
John T. Fielding
Patrick H. Forson
William Forson
James R. Fuqua
James T. Given
William Cooper Goff Jr.
Thomas Samuel Goodbread
Burwell K. Greene
Rowland Hair
Silas Hatch
Thomas Henry Hawkins
James A. Hodge
Archibald Hurst
Luke M. Jenkins
Alexander L. Johnson
James Johnson
Joseph Jones
Robert Wiley Kelly
Baxter M. Leach
Jesse Lee
Gideon Locklier
John Locklier
William Locklier
Thomas Low
George W. Martin
Zachariah B. Mathers
Charles McClellan

James Pinckney Morgan Sr.
Benjamin F. Owens
Owen W. Parker
Walter Miles Parker
James Alfred Peacock
James W. Rawls
Thomas A. Reese
Henry Franklin Simmons
Moses W. Simmons
John L. Smith
Lovett B. Smith
Robert R. Smith
Simeon A. Smith
Thomas Swinner
Benjamin A. Tedder
Thomas R. Tedder
Benjamin R. Walker
George P. Walker
James M. G. Walker
William T. Walker
Byrd Watley
George Wright
Needham Yates
Gideon Yorklier

COMPANY I

Capt. Nicholas S. Cobb
Lt. Henry Bradford
Lt. John W. Nash
Lt. John G. Rawls
Lt. George W. Dell
Lt. Burrell Thomas Stokes
1st Sgt. Thomas Starling
2nd Sgt. James T. Weeks
3rd Sgt. James Henry Wilkenson
4th Sgt. Joseph B. Harrell
1st Cpl. Nathaniel J. Renfrow
2nd Cpl. John R. Hall
3rd Cpl. Sanders Nobles
4th Cpl. Daniel P. Holder

Company I Privates

Louis Appel
Robert D. Beck
Eli Hardy Benefield
James A. Brock
Lewis Berrian Daniels
Daniel J. Davis
William T. Dell
Henry Taylor Dowling

Arthur E. Everitt
Daniel David Faircloth
Sanford Faircloth
John Gaines
John Garner
Elijah Gibson
Andrew J. Giddings
John Grimes
Monroe D. Hagin
Isaac Highsmith
John F. M. Highsmith
Arthur J. Hodge
Garrett V. Hudson
James W. Johns
Louis J. Johns
Archibald E. Kelty
George S. Leavett
Jessey Lofton
Edward Long
Levi Long
Andrew J. Lynn
Hiram Martin
Simpson McGehee
Alexander McLeod
Neil McLeod
Green Medows
James Parish
Tyre J. Parish
Thomas I. Pedricks
Anderson Philpot
James Jefferson Philpot
Thomas W. Philpot
Barnett Price
William Roddenberry
William Ship
Miles Shepherd
Wiley B. Sims
Henry Sparkman
James Starling
David . Strawn
James L. Strawn
Thomas C. Thorrington
Naon Tomlinson
William Tomlinson
Isham Walker
Landrick A. Walker
Uriah Walker
Richard J. Waters
Hosea White

James Thomas White
John P. Whitmore
C. Wilkerson [or Wilkinson]
J. H. Wilkerson [or Wilkinson]
Lewis Wilkinson
William R. Wilkinson
Willis Wilkinson
Cornelius C. Williamson
John Williamson
Stephen F. Williamson
William Williamson
Absalom B. Wood
Iggliah Nelson Wood
John B. Wright

COMPANY K

Capt. David Hughes
Capt. Gaston Finley
Lt. Emmett E. Barry
Lt. William Platt
Lt. William Hughes
1st Sgt. Andrew G. LaTaste
2nd Sgt. William M. Melvin
3rd Sgt. Robert J. Bradley
4th Sgt. John W. Tanner
1st Cpl. Samuel B. S. Harris
2nd Cpl. Stephen Hull
3rd Cpl. Hillary Tyer
4th Cpl. James West Futch

Company K Privates

William T. Adams
William W. Barber
Elbert E. Barker
William Riley Barker
Alexander Black
Nicholas A. Braswell
Joseph Brooker
James Calhoun
Benjamin F. Colbert
Fleming Colbert
Hampton Combee
James M. Cooper
Henry C. Crews
Micajah Crews
William A. Crews
William B. Crews
John William Crichton
John W. Darby
Thomas J. Darby

William Darby Jr.
Michael Henry Dickens
Charles W. Downing
Cornelius Drawdy
Benjamin F. Drew
William C. Drew
Darlington Fillman
William H. Futch
Rodolphus Garbett
Morris Giddeon
Harvey James Goddard
Iverson Godwin
Andrew J. Gold
Christie C. Gordon
David L. Harvill
William Charles Hawkins
William Marion Hendry
Thomas J. Holton
Edwin L. Hutchinson
Lewis M. Jenkins
George W. Kilpatrick
William Erastus McClelland
Samuel McKinney
James McNeill
James T. Miley
John Monroe
John North
Jerry Peede
Lemuel Peede
Allison W. Peters
George Harrison Peters
James Pharr
John T. Pollock
William M. Purvis
John Riols
James Roberts
Theophilus H. Rushing
John Ryals
Simon P. Smith
James Stafford
William Stafford
Allen Summerall
Erasmus M. Thompson
James C. Vanderipe
Josiah Varn
Andrew E. Wade
Elias Whiddon
Asa Whitehurst
Hopkins M. Wilder

The following persons, found in widow pension applications, family records, and various unofficial records, claimed to have served with the First Florida Cavalry Regiment, C.S.A.. However, efforts to document their service using the official records and rolls, have been unsuccessful. It is quite possible that at least a few may have served with the Union's First Florida Cavalry Regiment, or another Confederate organization. It is also possible that some may be duplicates of names listed in the official rolls, resulting from misspellings or misinterpretations on the part of the informational source. But, just in case they do belong in the Regiment's history, they have been included for reference.

John A. Allen
Lt. J. B. Barnum
J. C. Barromer
H. B. Blount
J. C. Blount
J. B. Borrow
W. L. Bush
W. W. Clements
Abraham Ganaur
J. Gaines
M. G. Gillis [or Gillas]
George Johnson
A. J. Jones
J. R. Joyner
J. Kasoutte
Willis A. Kent
F. A. Knowles
Albert Martin

J. C. McLeod
John McMillan
George McMullen
William R. McMullen
Sgt. L. B. McTyier
Willoughby Miles
John Miller [or Mollie]
J. Page [possibly Co. E]
Robert H. Parish
S. F. Pigot
J. Powell
J. E. Rowe
F. Stafford
Lewis B. Taylor
A. M. Vicker
Robert W. Walker
G. H. West
Cpl. A. J. Wood

SELECTED BIBLIOGRAPHY

I. BOOKS AND PUBLISHED WORKS

Davis, Thomas Frederick, *A History of Jacksonville, Florida and Vicinity 1513 to 1924*, Florida Historical Society: St. Augustine. 1924.

Dickison, John J., "Military History of Florida," *Confederate Military History*. 12 vols. Edited by C. A. Evans. Confederate Publishing Company: Atlanta, Georgia. 1899.

Johnson, R.U. and C.C.Buel, editors. *Battles and Leaders of the Civil War*, 4 vols. 1887-1869. Reprinted edition: Secaucus, N. J. n.d.

-----*Regulations for the Army of the Confederate States*, 1863. Republished by the National Historical Society: Harrisburg, PA. 1980.

-----*Revised Regulations for the Army of the United States*, 1861. Republished by the National Historical Society: Harrisburg, PA. 1980.

Robertson, Fred L., compiler, *Soldiers of Florida in the Seminole Indian, Civil and Spanish-American Wars*. Democrat Book and Job Print Company: Live Oak, Florida. 1903.

II. HISTORICAL PERIODICALS

Doty, Franklin A., ed. "The Civil War Letters of Augustus Henry Mathers, Assistant Surgeon, 4th Fla. Regiment," *Florida Historical Quarterly*, 36, {1957}: 94-124.

Havird, Aleene M., compiler, *A Tribute To William A. Cox, Confederate Soldier, 1841-1907*. [A family memorial publication] dated 1983.

Keen, Mary W., "Some Phases of Life in Leon County During the Civil War." *Tallahassee Historical Society Annual*, IV [1939].

-----Past Times, *125th Anniversary of the Northwest Georgia Campaign, a special supplement*, News Publishing Co: Rome, Georgia. 1989.

III. LETTERS, DIARIES, AND JOURNALS

-----"Diary of Henry McCall Holmes," University of Florida. Gainesville.

Cabaniss, Jim R., *Civil War Journal and Letters of Washington Ives, 4th Fla. C.S.A.*, 1862-1865, transcribed-published by J. Cabaniss, 1987.

-----"Hawkins Family Genealogical History," in author's possession.

Lee, Edmund C., "Civil War Letters," Copy of unpublished paper, Florida Historical Survey, 1937: Stetson University, Deland.

-----Merritt Family Genealogical Records, in author's possession.

-----The Letters of William and Julia Stockton, 160 letters and news clippings. 1845-69. Florida State Archives: Tallahassee.

-----Selected Confederate Soldiers Letters, 1861-65. Florida State Library.

----Papers of Francis P. Fleming, Florida Historical Society Library.

IV. NEWSPAPERS

-----*The East Floridian*, [Fernandina reference articles] 1860.

-----*The Floridian and Journal*, [various editions], Tallahassee, 1860-62.

-----*The Jacksonville Herald*, [assorted articles], 1865.

-----*The New York Times*, [Ref: W.G.M. Davis], December 1865.

V. PERSONAL NOTES, REFERENCES, AND SPECIAL STUDIES

-----Miscellaneous references and notes, [Ref: The Battles of Fort Myers, Resaca, and Bentonville, battle maps, etc],-contributed by Louise Sullivan.

-----Florida Civil War Flags, [informational letter in ref to the 1st Cavalry and 4th Florida combined regiments]. Curator, Museum of Florida History, Department of State: Tallahassee, Florida, 1997.

McCammon, Thomas A., "Interpretation of the Trial of William Lunt," [a private study and unpublished inquiry into the Lunt case] 1990.

-----Recollections from descendants of 1st Florida Cavalry veterans responding to genealogical queries published in *The Florida Genealogist*.

-----Selected items about William Cox of the First Florida Cavalry, contained in correspondence between Mr. Bill Cox and the author.

-----*The Confederacy* webpage, contains general Florida civil war military history and strategy, compiled by Charlie C. Carlson III, U.S. Army.

United Daughters of the Confederacy, Diaries and Letters of Confederate Soldiers, copied from the files of the Georgia Division 4. Georgia State Archives: Atlanta. 1942.

VI. OFFICIAL RECORDS AND REPORTS

-----*Compiled Military Service Records of General and Staff Officers of the State of Florida*, microfilm series 989, Reels 1 through 5. Florida State Library: Tallahassee.

-----E. Kirby Smith Papers, Correspondence of General Smith, C.S.A., [1862 period military correspondence and papers]. Southern Historical Collection, University of North Carolina.

-----Florida Confederate Veteran Pension Applications. 1885-1954

-----Jefferson Davis Papers 1861-8165, official papers and correspondence, manuscripts division, Duke University.

-----Governor John Milton's Letterbook, official correspondence of the governor 1862-1865, Florida State Library: Tallahassee.

-----Muster Rolls of Florida Confederate Army Regiments. 1860-1865, consisting of 1st, 3rd, 4th, 6th Florida Infantry Regiments and the 1st Florida Cavalry Regiment. Microfilm reels. Genealogy Section, Public Library, Orlando, Florida.

-----Muster Rolls of Union Army Regiments, 1862-1864, microfilm reels, consisting of the 37th Indiana, 9th Maine, 57th Michigan, 35th, 37th, 53rd, and 174th Ohio Infantry Regiments. National Archives Branch, Atlanta.

U. S. Army Topographical Engineers, Campaign Maps, 1863-1865 Series, topographical surveys compiled for Dalton, Chickamauga, Bentonville, Dallas, Kennesaw, Nashville, and Atlanta areas: National Archives.

United States War Department. *Official Records of the Union and Confederate Navies in the War of the Rebellion.* 30 vols. Government Printing Office: Washington D.C., 1894-1927.

United States War Department. *War of the Rebellion: A Compilation of the Official Records of the Union and Confederate Armies.* 128 vols. Government Printing Office: Washington D. C. 1880-1901.

VII. SECONDARY REFERENCES

Boatner, Mark M. III, *The Civil War Dictionary*, revised edition, 1988. Vintage Books, Random House: New York. 1988.

Boatner, Mark M. III, *Military Customs and Traditions*, David McKay Company Inc. Van Rees Press: New York. 1956.

Davis, Mary Lamar, "William G. M. Davis, Brigadier General, C.S.A.," *Floridians Distinguished as Lawyers and as Soldiers.* The Florida Law Journal V23, 1949: Jacksonville.

Military Letters in the Major William Footman files. 1862-64. [5 items] Military Records Branch, National Archives: Washington D.C.

NAME INDEX

For additional names see the muster roll beginning on page 73

Gorilla Families

Claudia C. Diamond

The Rosen Publishing Group, Inc.
New York

Published in 2001 by The Rosen Publishing Group, Inc.
29 East 21st Street, New York, NY 10010

Copyright © 2001 by The Rosen Publishing Group, Inc.

Book Design: Haley Wilson

Photo Credits: Cover, pp. 1, 8, 15, 16, 19, 20 © Wildlife Conservation Society; pp. 4, 12 © John Chellman/Animals Animals; p. 7 © Roger Aitkenhead/Animals Animals; p. 11 © Clyde H. Smith/Peter Arnold.

ISBN: 0-8239-8168-1
6-pack ISBN: 0-8239-8570-9

Manufactured in the United States of America

Contents

The Gorilla

Gorillas are the largest **primates**. Primates are an animal group made up of monkeys, gorillas, and humans.

There are three kinds of gorillas. They are all found in Africa. The mountain gorillas live in the mountains of central Africa. There are also two kinds of **lowland** gorillas that live in the **rain forests** along the western coast of central Africa.

Male gorillas can weigh over 450 pounds. Females weigh about 200 pounds.

5

What Gorillas Are Like

Gorillas are very gentle animals. Like humans, gorillas take care of each other and spend a lot of time with their families. Gorillas also need attention and friendship, just like people do.

In the wild, gorillas spend about half of their day finding and eating different fruits and plants. Gorillas move from place to place. They never spend more than one night in the same place.

Older gorillas watch over the younger gorillas, just like someone looks out for you.

A Gorilla Family

There are usually ten to twenty gorillas in a family. A family often has one or more male gorillas, several females, and several younger gorillas. Gorillas aren't fully grown until they are about ten years old. When a male turns ten, he leaves the family to start his own family. A new group forms when one or more females join the male that has left the group.

Gorillas live together in big families, just like some human families do.

The Leader of the Family

As a male grows up, a silver patch of fur appears across his back. This grown-up male is called a **silverback**. The silverback gorilla leads the whole family and **protects** it from danger.

The silverback gorilla makes all the choices for the family. He decides when they will wake up in the morning. He decides where they will go that day. He even decides when they will rest.

The silverback gorilla has an important job to do. He is in charge of the whole gorilla family!

A Day in the Life of a Gorilla Family

Gorillas wake up and begin eating soon after the sun rises. They eat **bark**, many kinds of leaves, and fruit. After this, the younger gorillas play. The adults rest until the middle of the afternoon. Then the gorillas eat again.

At night, gorillas use tree branches to build a new nest for sleeping. They usually build this nest on the ground, but sometimes they build the nest in a tree.

The younger gorillas play while the adults take an afternoon nap.

13

Learning How to Be a Mom

Young female gorillas learn how to be good mothers by watching the older mother gorillas raise their babies. A young female also helps take care of her younger brothers and sisters. She learns how to hold them and play with them. When she has her own babies, she will be ready to be a good mother.

This mother gorilla has learned how to be a mom by watching the older female gorillas raise their babies.

A Mother Gorilla and Her Baby

A baby gorilla is as helpless as a human baby when it is born. For the first few months of the baby's life, the mother holds the baby gently to her chest. She carries the baby wherever she goes. The mother's milk is the only food a baby gorilla can eat at first. As the baby gets older and stronger, it will start to eat foods like berries and leaves.

Gorilla babies need a lot of help and attention, just like human babies do.

As a Baby Gorilla Grows

A baby gorilla soon becomes strong enough to hold on to its mother by itself. It will often ride around on its mother's back, holding on to her fur.

A baby gorilla can crawl when it is about three months old. It can walk by the time it is five months old. However, the baby gorilla will still often ride on its mother's back until it is almost three years old.

A young gorilla can get a piggyback ride if it is too tired to crawl or walk.

19

What a Zoo Can Do

Some gorillas live in zoos. Zoos are safe places where people can look at **wildlife**. Zoos also save animals that are in danger of disappearing from Earth.

Gorillas are in great danger in Africa. People are destroying the **homeland** of the gorillas to clear land for farming. Zoos give gorillas safe homes. Zoos also give gorilla families a place where they can have more babies.

Zoos are safe places where baby gorillas and their families can live and grow.

The Fight to Save the Gorilla

Only about 50,000 lowland gorillas and a few hundred mountain gorillas are left in the wild. Laws have been passed to protect gorillas. **Poachers** continue to kill mother gorillas to get their babies. The poachers take the babies and try to sell them to zoos. Most zoos will not take these gorillas, and hope that this will stop poachers. Zoos around the world are working to save the gorillas.

Glossary

bark The outside covering of the trunk and branches of trees and bushes.

homeland The area that is someone's home.

lowland An area of land that is lower and flatter than the land around it.

poacher A person who illegally kills animals.

primate The group of animals that includes monkeys, gorillas, and humans.

protect To keep someone or something safe from danger.

rain forest An area that has a lot of rainfall every year.

silverback An adult male gorilla that is the leader of a gorilla family.

wildlife Animals and plants that live in the wild, far from humans.

Index

A
Africa, 5, 21
animal(s), 5, 6, 21

D
danger, 10, 21

E
eat(ing), 6, 13, 17

F
family(ies), 6, 9, 10, 21

L
lowland, 5, 22

M
mother(s), 14, 17, 18, 22
mountain, 5, 22

P
poachers, 22
primates, 5
protect(s), 10, 22

R
rain forests, 5

S
silverback, 10

W
wildlife, 21